True Stories from the Morgue

True Stories from the Morgue

JOHN MERRICK
Forensic Counsellor

For all those whom I have counselled.

Table of Contents

Introduction 9

1	Three little children	15
2	The day I was attacked	39
3	Catastrophe on the roads	55
4	Two sides of guilt: a suicide and a pool drowning	83
5	These foolish things ... my worst mistake	125
6	After hours at crime scenes	141
7	Hitting the wall	161
8	A child's brutal murder: A mothers response	187
9	A tragic crash; a young widow's nightmare	213
10	The Bali bombings	235
11	Expect the unexpected at an inquest	255
12	Little known facts about autopsies	271
13	A few more tales	295
14	Walking out of the morgue	307

Postscript 315
Acknowledgements 318
About the Author 319

INTRODUCTION

I spent the best part of twenty years working in a very unusual environment. When I say unusual, it wasn't because the actual office was strange or the people with whom I worked were unusual, it's just that it was not the type of work that many people do. I say this because I worked in the inner Sydney suburb of Glebe at the Institute of Forensic Medicine – the morgue.

I first started working there at the age of 29. I had had some experience as a social worker in hospitals, but the bulk of my experience until then had been working in a hospice caring for the terminally ill in the southern suburbs of Sydney. However, my very first job was at a hostel for homeless men in Kings Cross in Sydney. It was the place where I first really came across death and its repercussions. Some of the men developed cancer or a serious medical illness and would often stay there until near death. I

Introduction

spent time with these men talking about their lives, their regrets and they would tell me what they had experienced – tales often filled with alcohol, gambling and violence. When they were near death, they spoke about their fear. I visited a few in the local public hospital where they died.

At the hospice, I dealt with people nearing the end of their existence and I sat with patients and their families as the patient died. I felt comfortable in seeing dead people, but all the dead I had seen thus far had been from disease, usually cancer and often they died surrounded by loved ones in the relative peace of a place that specialised in dealing with the slow and certain outcome of advanced cancer. Most died pain free and were cared for by their families and some truly dedicated staff.

Then I got a call one day from a woman I had met briefly. She was the social worker at the Institute of Forensic Medicine and asked me if I wanted to work with her on a temporary basis providing counselling and support for those bereaved by sudden death. I didn't realise at the time, but this was going to be one of the turning points in my life. The year was 1989.

I was initially employed to do a short-term locum job for three to six months. Little did I know that I was signing on for almost two decades.

Introduction

I should make it unequivocally clear now that I am writing about the experiences of those with whom I worked and those I counselled during my time there. The stories are all true. I have changed the names in some stories to protect the privacy of the people. It is not my intention to humiliate or subject anyone to ridicule. I hope that sharing these stories will help others at some time.

I worked very closely with police, ambulance and fire officers, but much of my time was spent with forensic pathologists, my fellow counsellors in the counselling team, the State Coroner and the Deputy State Coroners. However, the group with whom I spent the bulk of my time with was the bereaved. I am truly grateful for having met them. I learned so much from them and passed on their lessons to other families, I believe helping them in some fashion.

To some of my colleague's shock and horror, I befriended a few of those I was counselling. I am still close friends with Christine Simpson, whose daughter Ebony was murdered aged nine in 1992. We still get together every year, drink too much red wine and eat too much food on the anniversary of Ebony's death.

I should mention the police. Most people's experiences of the police are when they have had a run in with the law, usually when they have been booked for speeding; in other

Introduction

words, when they're on the wrong end of a telling off or receiving a fine. The police, with whom I worked, were tireless, invariably compassionate and caring and were dedicated decent men and women. I had most contact with the officers from the forensic police unit and the homicide detectives who were really amazing people.

This book tells my story of my time working at the morgue. As a counsellor, it focuses on helping those left behind after sudden, unexpected death. This is my experience of what I did and what I saw, things that happened, things that went wrong, things that went right and about those with whom I worked when shocking things happened. I was at the morgue when two dreadful bus crashes in New South Wales killed many people. I was there for the aftermath of the Bali bombings in 2002 – another horrific incident that saw many Australians die in a single stroke. And there are other instances of sudden death from murder and suicide which are equally as devastating for their loved ones. Because I have had to rely on my recollections of conversations during my time as a forensic counsellor, the conversations retold in this book are as I remember them. They are therefore not 100 per cent accurate but I believe that they do convey the essence of the relationships I had with others, whether fellow workers, the police and other emergency workers and

Introduction

the bereaved.

I think I can look back at the work I did and be a little proud. I think I achieved some changes for the better during my time at the Glebe morgue. To my regret, I also did some things of which I am not so proud; but that is life. I know I have learnt from my experiences working there. Despite the nature of the work, we who worked at the morgue laughed a lot and cried some. I pay tribute to all who made this time what it was.

The term 'job' is a curious one and I use it in this book in a particular way. People often talk about their employment as a job or their job. When I use the term, I use it a little differently. For me, it is a term to describe a particular event during my time in the 'job' of forensic counsellor. When police talk about doing 'a job', they refer to an event in much the same way; a crime in which they were involved.

In the book, each chapter starts with the phrase: 'I did a job once when ...' It may be a job that relates to a car crash, a suicide, an infant's death. Members of the constabulary will often approach each other and say, 'How long have you been in the job?' They often are referring to something that happened within their day-to-day work. The term, job, then takes on a whole new meaning. I guess I adopted the term and use it to explain different jobs that I was involved in

Introduction

during my time in forensic medicine. The stories in this book are my stories about the jobs that I did at the morgue.

CHAPTER 1

THREE LITTLE CHILDREN

I did a job once where the size of the bier room was the problem.

According to Merriam-Webster's online dictionary, a bier is a stand on which a coffin or corpse is placed. At the Glebe morgue, we had a bier room; a small room divided into two parts by a small wooden partition. The partition was no more than one metre, or about the same height as the mortuary trolley that held the body. When a family member wanted to view their loved one, the trolley would be wheeled out of the cold storage area, a large walk-in fridge. The body would then be covered by a blue hospital blanket. We would place a sheet and a pillow under the head to give the appearance of someone at rest. The blanket would be folded around the neck to provide some dignity in appearance. The trolley would be then wheeled

Chapter 1

down a small corridor and into the back door of the bier room through a sliding door that was only just wide enough to allow the trolley to fit through. There was only enough room for one trolley but there was enough space for a family member to touch, embrace or kiss the deceased if they so wished.

One Sunday morning, I was watching a TV news program at home when the journalist reported the murder of three children in Sydney. We'll get this job, I thought. I decided to check to see if anything was known about the family. I called and found out that the kids had been admitted and the next of kin was the mother. I asked about the case and what was known at the time. I was told that the police had arrested a man, the mother's partner.

I asked for the police details and called them to find out if they had any concerns about doing a viewing on the kids by the mother. Contact with any bodies in homicide cases is generally forbidden prior to the autopsy. The police investigator told me there would be no problem with the mother viewing the bodies of her deceased children. The forensic police had already done their work and conducted all the necessary crime scene investigations. I was given the number where the mother was staying and I called her soon after. As usual, there was a gatekeeper; someone who is

Three little children

protective of the bereaved person and who vets calls coming in. I spoke to a woman who told me that the mother was unavailable and she would call later. I explained to her that I was calling from the mortuary and that the children had been taken there for a coronial investigation. Within a few short seconds, the mother came on the phone.

'What is happening with my kids?' she asked.

'They've been taken to the mortuary at Glebe. They're here at the moment.'

'What are you going to do with them? They're only children.'

'The coroner is going to decide tomorrow morning whether or not an autopsy is to be conducted. We will meet tomorrow with the specialist doctors, the police and the coroner to decide whether an autopsy will happen. Do you understand what an autopsy is?'

'I've seen TV shows. Is that when they cut them? Please don't cut them. They're my babies.'

'An autopsy is done by a specialist doctor, and yes, incisions are made by the doctor to determine what happened, to work out the cause of death. It's the same as any big operation by any doctor. I know that sounds really hard to hear but I think the coroner will want to hold autopsies on the children because criminal charges will be laid against the person who

Chapter 1

has done this. If we don't have medical proof of a cause of death, it is harder to make charges stick. Given that the person who did this will have a lawyer, we don't want the person to be released because of a lack of evidence. It's really important that we do our job for the sake of you and the children. But really, that's not my decision. The coroner will decide that tomorrow morning. When a decision is made, I'll give you a call if you like. You do have the right to formally and legally object to the autopsy if you wish but that involves the coroner formally ordering one and then you appealing to the Supreme Court for a ruling. That can take some time. But the decision is yours as the senior next of kin, their mum.'

'All right, I think I understand. When can I see my kids? Can I come in and see them?'

'Sure, that's fine. I'll find out when that can be done and I'll call you back in a few minutes. Is that all right? I just need to find out if anything else is happening. When would you like to come here?'

'Please call me back soon and let me know. I'd like to come as soon as possible. I want to see my babies. Please.'

Let me digress for a minute or two. I use the term 'viewing' in this chapter. It is when a family member comes to look at their deceased loved one; father, mother, husband, wife – you

Three little children

get the picture.

The viewing is often done at a funeral home but in coronial cases, the body is taken to a forensic mortuary. Families are often encouraged to wait for the release of the body which can take around three or four days, sometimes quicker. However, some people say that viewing a body is really important as it helps them to understand that the person is dead. 'Seeing is believing' is a term often used. In such cases, some family members come to the morgue to view the body of the deceased. In the case of homicides, this might have to happen after the autopsy. Generally, we were supposed to discourage viewings at the morgue, to encourage family members to wait until the body as at a funeral home – or that was the case during my time.

Viewing the deceased relative is a matter of choice. Some people choose not to, saying that they would rather remember the person who has died as they were. There are no right or wrong opinions here and people react very differently when they view a dead person. Some people are frightened, others hysterical, others find great peace in spending time with the person they loved. In my experience, I have found that a good viewing is very beneficial for those who chose this option. When prepared carefully, the experience can bring a certain sense of peace. On the other hand, a poorly done

Chapter 1

viewing can be damaging. You need to give people time to prepare, spend time with the dead and let them say a few words, maybe a prayer.

Before I worked in forensic counselling at the morgue, I was under the impression that if a body was disfigured, burned or badly traumatised, it would be ill advised to have the family view the body. I have changed my mind completely over time. I have seen family members view skeletal remains, badly burnt bodies, people who had been shot or have committed suicide and many other types of trauma. I vividly remember one case.

A young man was murdered and dismembered by the killers. His body parts were left in different locations, some never recovered. The young man's head was discovered in a bag near a river. The head was identified using dental records and his mother was notified. She rang me and asked if she could come in and see him. We only had his head. I initially refused the request, thinking that this was a recipe for further traumatising the woman. But she was a strong willed woman and would not take my refusal. I explained to her that we were only in possession of her son's head and that it would be very distressing for her. She was most insistent and contacted someone much higher up the food chain than me. Subsequently, I was told in very clear terms that I must

Three little children

agree to the request. So I did and the mother came in.

I have memories of the assistant placing the head on the trolley, held in position by a series of strategically-placed towels and blankets. Of course there was no upper or lower body, so it lay there on the trolley in isolation. Prior to the viewing, I explained to the mother what she would see in detail. She went into the viewing room and walked straight to her son's head and spent time there. She thanked me afterwards and explained that she now could really believe he had died and that she felt more at ease because she had done so.

This viewing helped me to understand that, if the preparation is sound and done well, people can gain benefit from seeing the person or their remains.

In the case of the three murdered children, I called work and asked whether any other viewings were scheduled. There weren't. I told the mortuary assistant I'd call him back to sort out a time for the viewing by the children's mother. Because only one trolley could fit in the room at a time, I would need to organise three separate viewings.

I called the mother to arrange a time then went into work late Sunday afternoon. The entrance workers use to the Glebe mortuary is small, a frosted glass door in a small street in Glebe off Parramatta Road. I rang the bell and

Chapter 1

went straight through to the fridge to have a look at the kids. The body storage area is large enough to accommodate hundreds of bodies. Most of the deceased are on trolleys on the floor, some of the boxes with skeletal remains are placed on a shelving system above the ones on the floor. For privacy sake, bodies are placed in body bags and the bags are sealed and resealed following any viewing or after any medical procedures.

I spoke with the assistant on duty and he was ready to prepare the kids for viewing. He had blankets ready to lay on top of the kids and three sheets to place under their little heads. The mortuary assistant told me one of his kids was the same age as the eldest. I could see his anguish at the thought. I just nodded. What can you say to that? Kids aren't supposed to die this young and in this way. I thanked him for the preparation he had done and we had some time so we went outside for a break. We spoke about everything else except the kids. We both wanted to speak of them but we didn't. Instead, we pretended that nothing was wrong, that nothing was unusual; except for three murdered children.

The mother arrived and buzzed to be let in. She was accompanied by a couple, obviously her friends who had come along in support. I ushered them into the small anteroom that was directly connected to the viewing room.

Three little children

Within the room, I had wheeled in the trolley with the body of her eldest daughter, unbeknown to mum who was seated only about ten feet away. I always prepared people before a viewing. It is really important to give them a chance to have some understanding rather than just blundering in and not knowing what to expect. I had done this many times before and I felt comfortable in describing what the mother and her companions were about to see.

'Through the door just behind us, there is a small room. It's a light coloured room but quite dimly lit. In the middle of the room there is a small partition. Just behind the partition, there is a hospital trolley. Your daughter is on the trolley. I've put a blanket to cover her and we've put a sheet behind her head. She has her eyes closed. She will feel very cold to the touch and a little damp. We have to keep people under cold conditions here. You can kiss her, or touch her, hold her hand if you like. I'll come in with you and then if you would like to stay by yourself for a while, that's fine.'

I always said something similar and I always said it slowly, pausing at the end of each point.

'Please can I see her now,' was the only thing the mother could say.

She looked at me her eyes pleading; a broken woman, a woman whose life had been shattered by the death of all her

Chapter 1

children. I led her to the door and slowly opened it, allowing her the opportunity to look in before she entered. She was past me and at the partition in an instant wailing, 'Oh, my beautiful, beautiful girl. I'm so sorry. I'm so, so sorry.'

She stroked her hair and touched her cheek, bending over the partition to kiss her daughter. 'Oh my darling girl, oh my love,' was all she could say.

I stood back and leaned against the wall and watched her. I sometimes encouraged people to touch, to kiss or embrace the body. This mother needed no such encouragement. Women, on the whole usually want to touch, kiss and caress; men are usually more reserved, sometimes needing prompting to get close. She stood by the partition, stroking her daughter's hair, tears flowing and her shoulders heaved as she stood there.

There was no need for me to say anything. The words would have been useless anyway. What can you say to a mother whose children have been taken away so cruelly? There are no words of comfort that I could provide. She stood there for some time. I can't tell how long, but the room became quiet as she stroked her daughter's hair and kissed her daughter. 'Thank you, John,' she whispered. I could barely hear her so I walked up to her alongside the partition. 'Thank you, John,' she repeated. 'Can I see the rest of my

Three little children

kids now?'

'Sure,' I said. 'I'll arrange that now. I'll take out your daughter and then come back with your son.'

'No, please, can I see my kids all together? They were always together so can I see them now together?'

'I'm sorry, but I can't fit more than one trolley at a time. Each one of your kids is on a separate trolley.'

'Please, please, I beg you to have my kids with me here together. Please, please!'

'I'm not sure what I can do, but give me a few minutes and I'll see if anything can be done.'

With that, she turned back to her daughter as I left the room. I didn't think that anything could be done but I guessed that, if I gave the impression that I had considered it, it might be enough. I walked back into where the assistant was sitting and told him that the mum wanted to have all the kids in the room at the same time. Of course, he said that wasn't possible because of the space issue in the viewing room. I walked to the body storage area to wheel the next child into the viewing room. One of his eyes was slightly open and this could often be disconcerting for a family member so I just held his eye closed for a minute and it remained shut. I wheeled the trolley to the outside door of the viewing room and heard the mother through the door. 'I

Chapter 1

want you all to be with me for one last time. I hope that John can help us to do that.'

I walked away. What the hell can I do? I can't do it. There's just not enough room. I grabbed the trolley and wheeled it back into the area outside the body storage room. I walked around to the anteroom before going inside the viewing room. There were about six chairs in the room and I stopped in my tracks. No, it wouldn't work, would it? I could try though and that would help the mum. Could I put the kids in chairs and prop them up with pillows? Maybe that would work. It seemed so strange on the face of things; to put dead children into chairs and prop them up with pillows.

It was a radical solution, to take the bodies off the trollies and prop them all in chairs, but it was worth a shot. I decided to speak to the mother to see what she thought of the idea. I gently opened the door; she turned around expectantly. She smiled at me, a sad smile, her eyes red from crying. I have to make this work. I have to, for her sake. I have to make it work.

'Ok,' I said. 'I think I have found a way I can get all the kids in here at the same time but it's a little unusual. Come and sit down in the room next door and I'll explain. She turned around and stroked her daughter once more. 'I'll be back soon darling. I'll just be next door.'

Three little children

She walked towards me and, at the door, glancing back at her child. She faced me as she went through the door and held her hand on my elbow.

'I knew you could do something John. I knew it,' she said.

I sat down opposite her and she held my gaze as we looked at each other. Her eyes were glistening but expectant.

'Look, this is what I have thought. I can't bring another trolley into the room. The room is just too small. So what I would like to do is bring the kids in one at a time and seat them in these chairs. I'll move the chairs into the viewing room and I'll carry the kids in and put them into the chairs and then we'll have all the kids in the same room at the same time.' My voice trailed off somewhat, unsure as to what she would say or think. She nodded.

'Yes, that would be great. I can have all my children with me once so we can be together once more, one more last time, one more time.' She bowed her head and started to cry once more. Tears rolled down her cheeks. I leaned forward and held her hands as they were folded on her lap.

'Yes, I can do this and you can have this last time with your kids together. Yes, we can do this.'

I smiled at her as she looked up into my eyes. 'Let me get started. I'll bring the chairs in first. Can you hold the door open for me, please?'

Chapter 1

She held the door open as I picked up the chairs one at a time and placed them close to each other in a semi-circle in the viewing room. Four chairs. Mum's chair was closer to the middle so she could see all her kids at the same time.

I walked back through the office and into the area just outside the body storage area. 'Are you done with the kids yet?' enquired the mortuary assistant.

'Not yet. I've got to do something a bit weird but I hope it will help the mum. You might think it's a bit left of centre. I'm going to put all the kids in the viewing room at the same time. I'm going to prop up the kids in chairs.'

'Really? Well, I guess she wants to say goodbye to the kids her way, so why not? I'm not worried, go your hardest! If you want a hand, sing out.'

'I'll be in the meal room,' he called as he walked off, seemingly not a worry in the world. The two remaining children were on trollies side by side. Ok, first the pillows. I grabbed a bunch of pillows and walked back into the viewing room, placing them on the chairs to form a slight hollow where the kids could be seated. I did a few trips, back and forth. Mum was with her daughter, and she would glance up and smile at me, not saying anything. She would be murmuring something to her daughter and whispering. I caught the odd word. 'Darling, my love, I'm sorry,' she

Three little children

whispered as she stroked her damp, cold hair.

Finally I was ready.

'Can I speak to you for a minute please,' I ventured. 'I need to put on a hospital gown and I don't want you to be surprised or alarmed when I carry the kids in. I just need to wear it as sometimes there is some moisture from people that have died and I need to just protect my clothes. Is that ok?'

'Yes, of course, that's fine,' she agreed with a sad smile. I decided I would first carry the eldest girl, so I went around to the back door and slid the door open. Mum was there looking at me.

'I'm going to pick her up and bring her round, ok?' She nodded. I told her to take a seat and pointed to the chair I thought she would be best placed. In my work at Forensics, it was rare that we actually carry bodies. I know that sounds trite to say, but as I slid my arm under her knees and the back of her shoulders, I felt like I was about to carry a living child, one that could be harmed if I dropped her or inadvertently caused her pain. This is patently ridiculous, but it's what I felt. I felt protective of this little girl. I should not drop her or be rough. I need to be careful and treat her carefully. I lifted the little child into my arms, shouldering her weight. I had to move my arms a little closer as her head could not provide

Chapter 1

support. I moved my arms under her shoulders and her back and as I did so her head tipped back sideways and onto my chest. It was almost like the times when I carried my own kids; when I carried them to bed after they had fallen asleep in the car, carrying their little forms and gently placing them in bed. Yet I could feel the cold from her forehead through the gown, a damp spot that grew colder as I walked through the office.

As I approached the door to the viewing room, I realised that I did not have a spare hand to open the door. I lifted the girl in my arms and tapped on the door with my elbow. As I did so, the girl shifted ever so slightly towards me as I lifted my arms to knock on the door. It was almost like she was coming closer towards me. The door swung open and mum's eyes lit up. 'Sorry John, I should have opened the door sooner. She's not too heavy, is she?'

'No, of course not. She's a lightweight like her mum.' I smiled. I bent down to place the child in the chair. I had to place her in the hollow I had created with the pillows and ensure that her head did not roll forward too much, or dip suddenly. I pulled the blanket up to her chin and folded it a few times so her head rested on the folds of the material. The pillows stayed in place and didn't collapse horribly. The girl looked as though she had fallen asleep with her head

Three little children

slumped forward. Her arms were covered as were her legs. Mum leaned forward from her chair and gently pulled back the blanket around her arm and softly caressed the little girl's arm down to her hand.

'She's cold to the touch, isn't she?' I said softly.

'Yes, so cold. She never liked the cold. She always wanted a second cover, a blanket,' she whispered softly more to herself than to me. She just stared at her daughter as if trying to will her back to life, as if it were possible.

I turned back through the door to start carrying in the other kids. I slid my arms under the knees and shoulders of one child. I performed the same routine as I had for the first, holding the body close to me for fear of dropping him onto the tiled floor. Again, the little damp head rested against my chest as I carried him quietly through the office and into the viewing room. Mum turned around as I entered and her face was the silent scream of a mother who lost everything.

I bent and nestled the child into the chair, pulling the blanket up and folding it so the child's head would not lean too far forward. Mum immediately rose from the chair and kneeled in front of the boy, lifting the blanket so she could stroke his arm. She rose from her haunches to kiss his face, her tears flowing freely, but she was silent. It was almost like the sound had been switched off, muted, as she kissed and

Chapter 1

stroked the boy's face and hands. In that moment, that very brief period of time, I did not move, stuck to the spot, not daring to disturb the intensely private moment of interaction between a mother and her dead son. I'm not sure to this day why I didn't move but I stood there and watched. I don't know how long I stood there, but it was probably no longer than a minute. I turned quietly and went for the third child.

Within a couple of minutes, I had returned and placed the child in the remaining chair. There were four chairs, three of them occupied. The chairs had their backs to the entry door, facing the wooden partition. I moved around and leaned against the partition, a silent witness to the mother's desire to have her children united. I took in the scene as mum quietly went from child to child, whispering words of love and of loss.

'I'm sorry my lovely boy, I didn't know he would be this way. I'm so sorry.' She repeated this to the children, interspersed with bouts of sobs. As I watched this scene, I had a sense that this was like some sort of still life painting. Unmoving children propped on chairs by pillows and blankets, their mother the only source of movement as she, at times, crawled from one child to the next. At one stage as mum kissed one of the children, the little body began to fall forward. I then stepped quickly forward and stopped the child from falling

Three little children

onto the floor. 'It's all right, I gotcha,' I said to the child. 'Oh, I have to be careful,' mum said through her tears. I returned to my spot and watched again.

The little faces had formed beads of condensation that really looked like they had been sweating, just like after exercise. They were so still. The slightly dim light in the room made it all seem like a dream sequence. Mum still moved between the kids, and then all of a sudden, she stopped and turned to me. She stood and walked towards me. She was much shorter than me, her head barely reaching my shoulder. She raised her arms and wrapped them around me and rested her head on my chest. 'Thank you, John. You are a good man. Thank you so much for this time with my babies.'

'That's ok. I'm really pleased we could help you. I'm so sorry for your loss,' I ventured. 'If you would like more time, I can arrange it. It's no trouble really.'

'No, I'll leave now. I'll just say goodbye to them and then leave, because if I don't leave now, I never will.' She smiled a sad smile. Mum returned to each child in turn and said her goodbyes. She turned at one stage and looked at me. 'This one feels the cold,' she said. 'Can you get a second blanket for her when you put her back in the cold room? I would really appreciate it.'

Chapter 1

'Of course, I can do that. No trouble.' I meant it too. I made sure I placed a blanket on the child when I returned her to body storage. We sometimes had requests like that. People would say that the deceased felt the cold and would we place a blanket on them. Whenever we had a request like that, we always did it, no matter what.

'I have to go now. I'll see you soon,' she whispered as she walked to the door turning and blowing them a kiss. I shut the door behind us, leaving the children behind.

'Please sit for a minute or two before you go,' I suggested motioning her to the remaining chairs in the anteroom. 'You've got friends to take you, haven't you? It's really important to have someone around you can talk to at times like this. The couple outside will care for you?'

'Yes, they're good people. I am staying with them and they'll drive us back to their place. Can you please call me in the morning and let me know what happens with the coroner? I'd like to know if that's ok. Now, what do I do about a funeral? What am I going to do about that?'

'All you need do is call the funeral director of your choice and they will liaise with us about the kids. They will take care of everything for you. Just call them tomorrow or the day after and they'll come and see you at your place or you can go see them. No rush.'

Three little children

She stood up and embraced me once more. 'Thank you, thank you. Please look after them for me, will you?' I nodded and said 'I'll call you tomorrow around nine after the meeting, ok?' She nodded as she walked towards the door. I opened the door for her and she slipped through, looking around for her friends. The couple were sitting in a parked car and she walked towards them. I never saw her again.

I turned and went back into the viewing room. The little figures sat there like statues, and I stood for a few seconds looking at them all in a row. I scooped up one child after the other, placing them back on the mortuary trollies. I made sure I put the blanket on the little one who felt the cold.

As I left, I made the usual vague cheerio to the assistant on the way out. I had parked in the garage. I opened the car and sat in the driver's seat and fiddled with the keys. I looked down at my shirt and noticed a damp spot, just on my chest. It was dark and round in shape. I thought for a second and remembered three little heads that rested against my chest.

I have rarely shared this story. I'm really not sure how people will react to the fact I placed three dead children in chairs so their mum could spend time with them. It's almost like dead people are supposed to lie down, and not sit in chairs like the living.

Chapter 1

I was once in the company of a very experienced social worker and began to tell her what had happened. She just threw up her hands and told me to stop; that it was too horrific to hear what I was saying. She might have even looked at me with an element of disgust. I immediately stopped the narration and walked away.

However, I often think back on the event with the mother and her three dead children and question myself. I know that the time spent in forensics affected me and changed me as a person. I saw and did things that people would not begin to understand. Maybe I had become so acclimatised to dealing with death that I thought what I was doing was normal. Maybe I am some sort of freak that places children in chairs when they should be lying on mortuary trollies. Well, maybe I am strange and maybe doing that was breaking some sort of social taboo. As I said, I've almost never told this story. Maybe I am aware that people would judge my behaviour, think me callous or extreme. Maybe that's why I don't share the story.

Actually, that's not the case at all. I remember that mother's face to this day. I remember her moving between each small shape like a spectre, kissing and embracing her children. I remember her smiling at them, loving them; I remember it all. I remember her gratitude. She thanked me

Three little children

and embraced me. She had said that she had valued the time and appreciated my efforts. So, maybe I bent some rules. Maybe I shouldn't have done it. Maybe I should have told her there was no way that the kids could fit into the room at the same time. But I don't think so. I did the right thing. To hell with the rules. I would do the same again in a heartbeat.

I spoke with mum the following day. She sounded tired, emotionally drained from the horrors of the last few days, from the hours of crying, from the feeling of despair she would face over the years to come.

That was the last time I spoke with her. Now, this admission hangs over me. Why didn't I maintain contact? Why didn't I counsel her? Why didn't I make sure she was cared for and supported?

The answer is not simple. We were a small team. At that time, there was virtually no support for people requiring this type of counselling. The Homicide Victims Support Group was yet to be created and there were very few counselling services that helped people in this situation. I didn't pursue any follow up for her, nor did I think much about the experience until now. Sometimes we need a sense of finality, an ending that can bring some sense into what is a senseless act. In many ways, I wish I could tell you how this woman fared, how she lived, her capacity to cope when hope is all

Chapter 1

but gone.

The truth is I don't know how she turned out, whether she is still alive, still grieving and coping with life following the death of her children or if she too has died. I do know that her partner was sentenced to prison for his appalling acts. I didn't attend the trial. Often trials are held years after the murders. By the time of the trial of the murderer of these children, I had moved on counselling many others and trying to make a difference as best I could; trying to keep up the frenetic pace that was my life as a forensic counsellor at the morgue.

CHAPTER 2

THE DAY I WAS ATTACKED

I did a job once when I was king hit by the deceased's relative.

The particular day when I was attacked was a Sunday. Around midday, I received a page. It was the Westmead mortuary asking for my assistance. A young Tongan male had died suddenly in what was potentially a homicide investigation. I spoke with the mortuary assistant on duty.

'What's the go with family?' I asked.

'There's a large family wanting to come to view the young bloke. I think there's a large group coming and I'd like you to come do the viewing if you can. I told them I'd give them a bell to come in once I got hold of you.'

'Ok, no worries give them a call and tell them three o'clock. I'll be there by then.'

The drive from my place to Westmead was about 50 minutes. I arrived early as I wanted to see how the body

Chapter 2

looked before seeing the family. I had some dealings with Islander families before. They were always unfailingly polite and decent, always very friendly and never aggressive. They often liked to sing songs as they viewed the deceased and I always found this quite beautiful. The songs were sometimes traditional and sometimes hymns. Still, I always liked it as they sang loudly and with great gusto. I said hello to the mortuary assistant and immediately went to the viewing room.

The young Tongan man was there on the mortuary trolley and his eyes were closed. He had some slight lacerations on his chin and above his left eye. He also had some discolouration above his left eye that looked like it might be a bruise. There had been some sort of altercation and, according to the police report, he had walked away seemingly fine. He collapsed a few hours later and died suddenly. The police report said that death was likely caused by a slow bleed from a head injury.

The police report, or the P79A as it was known, is the report of a death to the coroner. It is a form that contains identifying details of the deceased, next of kin details and a narrative surrounding the circumstances of death. The narrative often contained some rather interesting phrases such as 'the deceased got up from his chair to make a cup of

The day I was attacked

tea. The deceased then fell down during his tea making or the deceased entered his car. The deceased then drove into a tree. The impact caused the deceased to become deceased due to his injuries.' I often imagined the deceased rising up from the dead, Lazarus like, and making a tea or driving a car. Anyway, in this instance, the circumstances were seemingly suspicious due to the altercation that had taken place just hours prior to the death.

In cases like this, it is generally advisable that the family does not have physical contact with the deceased as their touching may contaminate the physical evidence that may be relevant to the prosecution. It is my job to explain to the family that it is important not to touch the body in any way until after the autopsy. Kissing, stroking and any other contact is not allowed at this point in time. I explain to them that doing so could affect evidence gathering and they could possibly compromise an investigation with their handling of their family member. I had said this previously to numerous families and was comfortable doing so.

The 'no touch' rule may warrant some explanation. I was told this story by one of the forensic dentists and he assured me of its authenticity. Sometimes a family member may be the offender. It is true to say that there are more deaths due to domestic-related homicides than stranger danger cases

Chapter 2

where an absolute stranger murders someone completely unknown to them. One example is that of the death of a young child reported to the coroner. His body had been brought to the mortuary. The family requested a viewing and during the viewing, a family member tried to place an object into the throat of the dead child in a vain attempt to make the investigators believe that the child had died from choking. The assistant, however, had seen what was happening and the family was removed from the viewing room. The police later charged two family members with murder. This attempt to compromise the investigation failed. Even so, a request to touch the body before an autopsy when a death is deemed suspicious is nearly always refused. The advent of DNA testing and the use of swabs and the like made touching the body a dangerous practice.

The family of the young Tongan boy – a large extended family – arrived to view the body. The bell rang in the mortuary foyer and I headed for the waiting area to let them in. In times such as these, I usually have the most immediate family members come in first, followed by the other members and friends. I opened the door and saw about twenty people, all Tongan by appearance, ranging from women in their forties to young children who would have been barely five or six years old. The three women closest to the door marched

The day I was attacked

straight past me and into the foyer.

'Hello, my name is John. I'm the counsellor here and I'm here to do what I can to assist you.' I smiled and welcomed them with a gesture, my arm waving them to enter the foyer.

'Where is he? I want to see my boy and I want to see him now,' said one of the women, a largish woman who held her handbag tightly as if I were going to grab it. Her eyes challenged me and I immediately realised that she was angry, very angry.

'Well, where is he? I want to see my boy. I don't want no counselling. I just want to see him and my family will come in too!' Her voice was harsh, authoritarian in a way. All the same, there was a pain behind her eyes that the bereaved cannot hide. It's always the eyes. Two other women from the group patted her on the shoulders and rubbed her back in an attempt to calm her.

'Sure, of course you can. That's no trouble. But there are some things I need to explain to you before you see him. I'd like to take you into the room just over here.' I motioned to the anteroom door. 'We can sit there and I'll explain a few things before we see him, ok?'

The anteroom was small, only enough room for four or five chairs. A door led from there through into the viewing room. The viewing room at Westmead was a smaller version

Chapter 2

of the one at Glebe. At Westmead however, a glass window separated the family from the deceased. There was a door that could be opened alongside the glass window, although in this case, the door was shut and locked. The circumstances around this young man's death were such that the family could not touch the body. At least that's what I thought at that moment.

'Please sit down,' I said, indicating the chairs to the three women. 'Firstly, can I make sure who you are please? I'm John, and you are …?'

'I'm his mum,' said the middle woman, 'and these are my sisters. My name is Losa and this is Oni and Lave.' She nodded to one then the other. The two nodded solemnly at me.

'Thanks. I just need to talk you through a few things before we see him. Now, your son is just in the room to my right, just over there. He's lying on a trolley and I've covered him with a blanket. His eyes are closed. He has what looks like a bruise above his eye and there are a couple of abrasions, scratches on his chin. When we go through, you'll see him behind a glass window. The thing is, when you see him today, I'm afraid you won't be able to touch him. You see …'

Mum's eyes suddenly flared, her face turned red. 'I want to see my boy and kiss my boy. You're not going to stop me

The day I was attacked

saying goodbye properly. I want to kiss him and touch him. Now stop talking and let me see him. My family and me are going to see him and touch him. You don't own him. We've got rights you know. Just let me see him …'

'I am really sorry but touching him may affect any evidence we can gather when we do the autopsy. Because of the circumstances, we need to limit people touching him and possibly removing some evidence that might lead to whoever did this being charged and found guilty. We do this so when the case goes to court, we can do the very best for both you and your family and your son. You see kissing him or touching him may affect what happens later when we do the medical testing at autopsy.'

This wasn't going well I thought. Usually the idea that someone might escape conviction because of their touching stopped people from doing so; maybe not this time. I carried on regardless.

'When we release him in a few days, you can spend more time with him and kiss and caress him when he is at the funeral home. There will be no troubles then with you spending as much time as you like. He will also be able to wear his own clothes and will look better than he does now.'

She looked at me as if I were her very worst enemy, a look that would inspire fear in anyone. She just stared at me and

Chapter 2

then she began to slowly shake her head. Her sisters looked at her, still patting her back and looking at her. She still just shook her head.

'Have you got kids? Do you know what its' like to have kids? Well?' she challenged.

'Yes, I do,' I responded gently. 'They're younger than your boy.'

'Well then, you must know how much you love your kids, how much they mean to you, what it would be like if something bad happened to them.'

'Yes, I love my kids and they mean the world to me. I can't imagine what it would be like if something happened to them. I'm so sorry for your loss. I'm really sorry that I can't allow you to touch him at the moment. It's just that I don't want you to be responsible for affecting any evidence. I just don't want you to regret anything you do today.'

'How can you be so cruel like this? How can you be so cruel when you have kids yourself? We aren't going to stuff up any evidence. We know what happened. We don't blame the other boy. It was just boys mucking around and it was real bad but I just want to see, I just want to touch him. He's my boy. You're not stopping me.'

'Look, we can talk some more after you have seen him. Why don't we go in now and we can discuss this a

The day I was attacked

bit later, ok?' I rose from the chair, looking at the dead man's mother. Her eyes never left mine. I was clearly her archenemy. She had a look that would have killed just about anyone.

I turned toward the door to the viewing room and probably took about two steps before I felt it – a stinging blow. I felt something hit the right side of my head. I had no idea at the time what it was but I fell. I dropped to my knees facing away from the women. I knew instinctively I had been hit. I shook my head and put my hand up to the side of my head. It stung and I could feel the heat starting to build where I had been struck. I lifted myself to one knee and swung around to face the women. The mother was being restrained by her two sisters, both of them struggling to hold on to her arms. She was struggling to get to me again.

'See? You see. I told you I want to see my boy, you bastard! You aren't going to stop me. You're not going to stop me. Now let me through. I'm gunna' see my boy. I'm gunna' cuddle him and hold him and you're not stopping me.'

I just looked at her and spoke as calmly as I could. 'All right, please stop. Please stop,' I said. 'I said you couldn't touch him but I see you're very angry and very upset and you have hit me. I can't let that happen again. I need to consult with the police and I will come back in the room and we will

Chapter 2

talk more. Let me see what I can do, ok?'

I needed to buy some time so I thought this tactic might hold her for a while. I held up my hand as in mock surrender – well, maybe it wasn't a mock surrender. Maybe it was the real deal; I was surrendering. I still held up my hands as I stepped carefully past the three women. The two women still held onto their sister as I slunk past. I don't think it was for her safety; it was more for mine. I went straight out the back of the mortuary and tracked down the assistant on duty. I found him watching TV in the staff room.

'Bloody hell,' I ventured. 'That wasn't fun.'

'What's up? Has the family finished yet? Can I put him away?'

'Not yet. I need to speak to the coppers on the case. You know, one of the family just belted me. Got me a beauty on the side of the head.'

'Fair dinkum? I'll call security. No, I'll call the cops. They can't do that. That's shit. I'll call the cops now.' He sounded as if he was the one who had been belted.

'No, don't call the cops. That's pointless. They're not going to charge anyone anyway. Which cop is going to arrest a bereaved mother?' There was silence from the assistant.

'His mother? The mother of the dead guy? The mother?' he finally blurted out.

The day I was attacked

'What are you? A parrot? Yes, his mother ...' My voice trailed off.

'One of the Tongan sheilas belted you?' You know when someone tells you a story and says it was so funny they almost wet themselves? Well this was such a moment. The assistant just began to laugh so loudly that I thought a pants wetting was a certainty. He began to snort he laughed so much. He doubled over and laughed some more. 'A sheila?' he said and laughed some more.

'All right, for God's sake. Will you shut up? Yes, she hit me and yes it still hurts, you bastard.'

'Sorry, John. I never expected you to come in here and say you were belted by a sheila. Don't worry. I won't tell anyone. And I won't ring the cops, ok?' He turned away still chuckling.

My face was red as much from embarrassment as from the blow. I went to get the paperwork on the young man and scanned for the police officer's details. I'll bet he isn't on duty today knowing my luck as I rubbed my face. Much to my surprise, he answered. After introductions I asked about the circumstances around the death. I enquired whether there would be a problem in allowing the family to touch the deceased. 'No, mate. It's all good. He was in hospital for a while so any evidence that might be compromised has

Chapter 2

been cleaned anyways. So yeah, that's fine.'

I thanked him for his time and turned and went back to see the assistant. 'It's ok for the family to go and touch the guy. I just spoke with the cops and they're fine with it. Unsurprisingly, he just looked at me and started to laugh again.

'Yeah, ok, whatever.' He turned back to watch TV still smiling. I stalked away. 'Bastard,' I said not terribly loudly.

I went back to the anteroom and the mum and her two minders were sitting there. All eyes fixed on me when I entered. 'Ok,' I said.

'Well? What did the police say? Can I touch my boy?'

'Yes,' I said blankly. 'The police said yes. I'm sorry for keeping you and making you wait. I've opened the door and now you can go in and kiss him and touch him. That's fine.'

'You see? I told you I would see him. I just love my boy and no one was gonna' stop me, no one!'

'Yes, I know. Especially not me. I'm very sorry that this happened today. Now, do you want to see him?'

I don't think they gave an answer, just went straight past me and into the viewing room, straight through the door and mum immediately kissed his forehead and held his hand she had retrieved from under the blanket. 'Oh, my poor boy. Oh, my darling.' She stroked his face and kissed him again. The

The day I was attacked

two minders stood alongside their charge and rubbed her back and murmured something I couldn't hear. I watched them for a while, but after a few minutes, I realised I was about as useful as a comb at a bald man's convention. I sat down and waited for them to finish. After a time, I walked back in and enquired as to whether they wanted me to let the remaining family in. Mum looked up and nodded. That was all.

As I drove home later that day, I thought about what had happened. I had not expected the blow and I had not expected the humiliation of the assistant's laughter that was still ringing in my ears. I felt hurt but mostly I felt embarrassed. Why was that? Was it ok for a woman to hit a man? It never crossed my mind to retaliate. I vaguely had thoughts of retribution but quickly dismissed them. Just get on with it, I decided. Big deal. So a woman hit you. She was big, though.

I arrived at work the following Monday and went to see the director. We often caught up to talk and he was always welcoming. 'How was the weekend?' he quizzed.

'Not great. I had a bit of trouble yesterday with a Tongan family. A young bloke died after an altercation with another young bloke. He collapsed and died shortly after. I told the family that they couldn't touch him for fear of contaminating evidence.'

Chapter 2

'Good work. The family can really do some damage to evidence when they're all over the body. Nice one.'

'Well, it doesn't end there. The family took the refusal badly and one of them belted me in the head.'

'What?' He just about exploded. ''I won't have my staff assaulted like this.'

He leant forward and picked up the phone. 'That's disgraceful. You were only doing your duty and they attack you. Were the police called? I'll ring up the Duty Operations Inspector and find out what's happening.'

'Leave it,' I said. 'Please just put the phone down.' He stopped and looked at me and slowly replaced the receiver.

'What then? What are you saying?'

'The person who punched me was the mother.'

'The mother? The mother of whom? The dead man?'

'Yes, the dead man's mother,' I said pronouncing each word clearly, 'the dead man's mother'.

'You're kidding, aren't you? The dead guy's mother gave you a slap and you're complaining. You want me to ring the police? Forget it.' He seemed angry with me all of a sudden. 'You let an old woman get the better of you and she belted you. Well, Merrick, I've never had a staff member coming to me complaining about being hit by a sheila but there's always a first time I guess. You let her punch you.'

The day I was attacked

He suddenly began to chuckle, followed by what I know now is a laugh although, at the time, he could have been having a convulsive episode. 'Ok Merrick, let's leave this between ourselves, shall we? I don't think your reputation is going to shine when people find out you were bested in combat by an old woman.'

'It wasn't like that. I had my back turned and I didn't see her …'

'Well, she still got the better of you.' He chuckled again. 'Get out. I've got work to do. See you later, Rocky.' I could hear him laughing as I walked off down the corridor.

During my time at the Glebe morgue, I met a lot of dangerous people including murderers and crooks but up until that time, I had never been assaulted. It took an angry mother of a dead man to teach me the value of watching my back. To their credit, neither the assistant at the Westmead mortuary nor my director ever let on what had happened. I still feel a bit shame faced about the whole episode but she did have a good right hook. I'll give her that.

CHAPTER 3

CATASTROPHE ON THE ROADS

I did a job once where we had to deal with the aftermath of two major vehicle crashes.

  I had only been working at the morgue for five or six months and I was still finding the work extraordinarily exciting and challenging. The deaths that occurred intrigued me and I was beginning to feel at home with the people and the workplace. To be honest, when I would go out socially, I would regale acquaintances with tales of murder and mayhem, ensuring of course I never mentioned specifics or identifying details. I loved the work and the work seemed to love me. I had found a niche where I really enjoyed the fast pace, working with the families of the deceased, and the difference I felt I could make and

Chapter 3

was making. I felt comfortable dealing with the dead and their stories.

Most days at the morgue, we deal with single deaths – a car crash, a hospital death, a suicide or a murder. Death usually happens in singles. It is rare for deaths to occur in any large numbers. At that time, none of our team had been involved in large-scale deaths. Most of the team who had been involved in the Granville train crash were no longer working. That crash on 19 January 1977 at Granville station in Sydney remains the worst train derailment in Australia. Eighty-three people died and 210 were injured. Some of the forensic pathologists were still working at the morgue, but no one in the counselling team where I worked. In fact, at the time of that crash, there were no counsellors employed at the Department of Forensic Medicine. However, it was not long after this horrific incident that counsellors were employed to support families doing viewings and identifications at the morgue.

So, there I was having worked for about six months and doing pretty well. I had developed really good relationships with the doctors and the assistants. Initially, the assistants had tried the usual round of practical jokes on me, as if to test me. The first 'joke' was shutting me in the body storage area. The large room is about three to four degrees Celsius.

Catastrophe on the roads

That's cold, very cold in fact. Even being shut in there for a few minutes is not pleasant. Of course, my colleagues all thought it a great joke. It was like an initiation; to see how I would fit in with them. After six months, I thought that I had passed the rites of passage and was feeling more confident in the role. All that was about to change with the devastating aftermath of two major bus crashes.

I don't remember getting a call or how I came to know about the first crash but I remember getting a team together so we could cope with the large numbers of dead. All I know is that a semi-trailer had sliced through a bus, killing twenty-two people, injuring numerous others. That crash had happened on the north coast of New South Wales near Grafton on Friday 20 October 1989 at around four in the morning.

To understand the enormity of the crash and what we would be facing in the morgue, it is important to explain a little about the nature of the crash itself. A semi-trailer truck travelling southbound at around 100 kilometres an hour veered into oncoming traffic colliding with a bus with 45 passengers onboard travelling at a similar speed. The impact of the collision was that the truck literally sliced through the bus opening it like a tin can causing catastrophic injury and death as many on the bus were torn apart. At the time, it was

Chapter 3

the worst road accident in Australian history.

I had witnessed dead with such injuries from car accidents that can leave people very battered, but never on such a magnitude. Since we had never really had to deal with such large numbers of dead people, we didn't know how to plan for the sheer numbers, nor how to actually do everything that needed to be done. We did know that each of the dead would need to be identified correctly so that we could deliver them to their families for cremation or burial. It was our responsibility to ensure we gave the right person back to the right family.

When I say 'our responsibility', I use the term loosely. The responsibility is really on the coroner. In a sense, we act as the coroner's arms and legs. The process of identifying the dead in large-scale disasters is called 'disaster victim identification'. It is a process that is quite prescriptive and involves the examination of the dead person and the collection of ante mortem information. In other words, this involves getting information about the dead person from family members; details such as height, weight, identifying details, name of dentist, tattoos, clothing worn, all sorts of identifying data that adds up to form a detailed description of the person. Naturally, these questions are on a specific form and it involves asking some very intimate details.

Catastrophe on the roads

In a single death situation of victim identification, a team is organised that includes a counsellor and a police officer to either visit the family or next of kin, to collect all the relevant information about the deceased. In this instance, when we had so many deceased, we needed to organise multiple teams so that all the victims could be correctly identified. Each team would need to contact a number of families of the dead that required team members to either travel to the family or have the family travel to the team. But we didn't have the number of people at the morgue to deal with such large numbers.

I spoke with my team leader, the other counsellor at the morgue, about how we were going to manage victim identification after the crash. She suggested that we call the senior social workers in each of the major hospitals and get their permission to use senior Emergency Department social workers to do these visits to family members. Strangely enough, we managed to get hold of all the seniors despite the fact it was a Saturday. I think people really wanted to help so were keen to make themselves available to come to Glebe.

We then needed to get the team of counsellors together which we managed to assemble at the morgue on that first weekend. I can't remember the numbers but there would have

Chapter 3

been about ten men and women who came in. They were all highly experienced in working with trauma in emergency departments but were novices when working with relatives after disasters.

There was a palpable sense of anxiety in the air as we spoke about their role in the process and the fact they would be spending time with families, mostly here at Glebe, with the odd one going to the family home of the victim. I don't need to detail the briefing, but there certainly were some anxious faces. I was the only smoker in the group but as soon as I went out into the courtyard, just alongside the briefing area, almost all of the counsellors came outside and asked for a sneaky cigarette. We sat outside, chatting amongst ourselves, not realising what we were about to face. We made sure we all looked very brave but I was feeling nervous for them as well as for myself.

A decision had been reached that the dead would be brought in to Glebe for identification using refrigerated transport. The trucks were parked overnight at a discreet location and driven early in the morning to the morgue. The reason why the dead from the crash were brought to the morgue at Glebe is that we were the only place with sufficient space for storage of so many bodies and the capabilities to conduct so many autopsies. The morgue is the specialist

Catastrophe on the roads

forensic facility with the expertise in forensic dentistry, and specialist teams making it the place where bodies are taken to do victim identification.

The first families of the deceased were due to arrive shortly after the trucks had delivered the bodies. The teams had been created by that time and the first team was told that a family had arrived. I distinctly remember the first counsellor going through the door to meet the family, looking back at me and smiling ever so slightly. I smiled back in reassurance. I was wondering how she would deal with the situation. I didn't know her at the time but I had been told she was a very experienced team leader at a major Sydney hospital. I thought she might need all her experience in dealing with the unknown scenario she was about to face.

I am sure that the family who arrived and the counsellor about to see them were unaware of the true extent of the tragedy. The family had been told that their loved one had died, but the circumstances would have been shadowy.

In today's world filled with mobile phones, computers, the Internet and social media, we can find out something almost instantly. Images of accidents and the like are posted from mobile phones. In 1989, we relied on television news reports and newspaper articles to find out what was going on. Such reporting often provided conflicting details. The extent of

Chapter 3

the disaster, the number of people who had died, who those people were – this information was sometimes incorrect. From the Grafton crash onwards, I learnt to await specific information before deciding on team numbers and briefing details. I found there was already too much panic without adding to it. To reduce that panic, every person on the team needs to be clear about their role, the job they each need to do and also what not to do.

Giving specific jobs to specific people is also important in such situations. I noticed how easy it was for people to be distracted and to start helping all over the place often where they were not needed and making other's work more difficult. I would see people performing all sorts of jobs, often at odds with what they were supposed to be doing.

I remember one of our team being stopped by another person and being asked to do something that was not one of her allocated tasks. She listened attentively and nodded seemingly eager to help wherever she could. I called out to her as she began to rush off. 'Can I have a word?' I called.

She stopped and turned to me with a questioning look in her eyes. She was a very caring woman who made her living caring for others in a very busy hospital emergency department. I had met her on a few occasions and was always impressed with her demeanour and her genuine compassion

Catastrophe on the roads

for people. I knew there was a risk of her being torn apart by competing priorities. It was my job to make sure that those in the team survived to fight another day. I didn't want them to be further victims of the absolute tragedy we were facing. She looked at me as if she had lost the power of speech. She opened her mouth and closed it again.

'Can we talk in the courtyard for a minute?' I ventured further. I don't usually like talking to people in the open space, but there was no other place at the time. We had used every single piece of real estate and there was nothing but outside space left. She followed me, utterly silent, her head a little bowed.

We sat on the cheap plastic chairs and I leant forward to get her attention. 'Do you know why I asked you to work here? Do you know why I think you are a great person to do this sort of work?'

'No, I'm not sure. I don't know why. You don't even know me. Why did you choose me?' She sounded as if something had broken inside. At this stage, we had been working since about six that morning and it was about three in the afternoon.

'I chose you because you are a very good social worker. I chose you because you seem to genuinely care about people. I chose you because you're the right person for the job. But,

Chapter 3

I think you're being ripped apart at the moment. You have too many demands on you as a person. I need you to stop.'

'I don't know what to do. I'm being asked to do too many things by people. The police are asking me ...' Her voice trailed off into silence.

'I know, I saw what was happening and that's why we're here now. That's why I said you're being ripped apart. I could see you were being asked to do a different job. I'm guessing the sort of person you are, you're going to find it hard to say no, especially if what they are asking is really reasonable. Yes, I think you're torn and that has to stop.'

She looked at me and tears welled in her eyes.

I went on. 'I'm sorry but I think I can help out, not just for the sake of the job, but also for your sake,' I whispered. 'It's vital that you do the job that's been allocated to you. You will do that job well and make sure it's done to the best possible standard. I expect that from you and I know you will deliver in the best possible way. When you don't have focus, you're going to get caught up in all the madness of this situation. When you lose that focus, you get torn and then begin to question what you're supposed to be doing and then get lost. I can't have that; I want you to still work here on this but I need you to be focussed and get back to the task at hand. Can you do that? Or the other option is that you can stand down and that's fine too. I need you to stay focussed on the job you have been given and not get seduced into taking on the responsibilities of others.' I smiled as she looked up and gave a slight laugh. 'Can you do that?'

'Yes, John. I want to stay and finish what we've started. I'm not ready to go home just yet. I guess I got caught up in trying to do too many things.'

'Yeah, I know and I understand that. I really understand that, but remember ...'

'Yes, I know, focus.'

'Exactly. Now, do you want to get back to work now or shall we have another ciggy for the road?'

She didn't hesitate. 'Shit yeah, I gave up last year but maybe just one.' We smoked in silence for a minute or two and then she walked off. I hope I did the right thing.

If there is one lesson I have learned from working after disasters, it is to stay focused. When I teach others about disaster situations, I always mention the need to be focussed, and how important it is to have role clarity. It is very easy to be distracted, to try to do too many things. The truth is, when people become distracted, they lose their capacity to work effectively. Taking on too many jobs can quickly lead to not doing the job allocated very well. It was a lesson I remember to this day.

Chapter 3

On that first morning when the dead started arriving, they were brought into the morgue and placed on the mortuary tables in the areas reserved for autopsies. Teams of police officers were photographing the dead and examining clothing, taking notes and completing the forms required to identify the deceased. These forms are essential with the police and forensic examiners completing half the form and family members completing the other. With both halves completed, we have an accurate identification. Of course, for this horrific crash, the process needed to be completed many times over. Because we had a passenger manifest, we at least had a starting point to identify who the victims were.

At the time, we did not do DNA testing as a matter of routine. In fact, the testing was not accepted practice then. Dental identification was generally used as this was very accurate and much quicker than using DNA testing. Dental ID involves getting the ante mortem records from the person's treating dentist, a task that was relatively straightforward once a family member has filled in their section of the identification form. The dental records are then compared to the records from the post mortem. The forensic dentists were phenomenal, often being pivotal to the correct identification of the deceased. They worked

Catastrophe on the roads

tirelessly with prolonged exposure to the mutilated dead, a task that was no easy feat.

I vividly remember walking into the autopsy suite after that crash. It is a large room that holds a series of stainless steel tables, each with its own sink, stretching out in tidy rows. This time however, each table held a victim from the crash. The sheer enormity struck me, as generally only eight or so tables might be use at any one time. On this occasion, all the tables were filled including fourteen in the main autopsy room and all the tables in the smaller autopsy room. Gripped in concentration the many assistants did their jobs with only the occasional comment being made.

'Turn him over now so I can see his back properly.'

'Yeah, that's good, thanks mate.'

'How's the picture? Good to go? Beautiful.'

I surveyed the scene, looking towards the back of the room where, on a table, there was an assortment of arms and legs waiting to be reunited with the correct body parts so that each body could be given a proper burial or cremation by family and friends.

It was a joyless task for the assistants; the same assistants who did this work with the dead on a daily basis. But this time it was on such a vast scale. I smiled at one of them as I walked down towards two guys I knew well.

Chapter 3

'How's it going?' I ventured casually.

'Just waiting for a break. We've been here since dawn. Just need a break to get out and have a coffee, or better still a beer.'

'Too right,' said his mate. 'Hanging out for one. This is thirsty work and its' been a long time coming. I feel sorry for him.' He motioned towards another assistant. 'He's got the two little kids. That's the worst part of this, the kids. Adults? Well, we get used to that. Kids, they're different for sure. Poor little bastards,' he said, his voice choking as he did.

'Yeah, it's shit. Everyone knows that. It's just shit,' I replied.

I was tempted to go and speak with the assistant who was dealing with the two children but I didn't. He didn't need to have to deal with me as well as what he had to do. I wouldn't have helped him at that stage by asking him how he was doing. I made a mental note to catch up with him later. That was another lesson I learned during this disaster; leave people alone when they are doing their job. Unless, of course, they want a break and want to talk. The sight of that room after the crash still comes to mind; seeing those men and women doing their sombre work which must have been difficult but of course, necessary. Maybe it was just the

Catastrophe on the roads

volume that was overwhelming. I'm not sure.

I have read books since that discuss the emotional responses and psychological consequences of working on disasters. The writings often mention the potential dangers of working in these situations; the possibility of stress-related conditions, the potential for developing post traumatic stress disorder (PTSD). I can see how people who are not used to dealing with this type of event can be easily affected. We know about soldiers who have fought in wars who suffer from the effects of PTSD – depression, feelings of worthlessness and sometimes, suicide. Working at the morgue can be similarly stressful. As a social worker and counsellor, I was well aware of this as was my team leader.

At the end of that first day, we decided that it would be a good idea to speak with all the counsellors – the social workers from the hospitals – at the end of their shift. We wanted to make sure they were psychologically together before going home to their families or partners. I sat with a few of them. Each looked a little ragged, unsurprisingly given the work they had done during a long day.

I started the conversation by enquiring how they had found the experience; in retrospect, a fairly preposterous question given what we were up against. Most replied that they were tired but that they were coping. I remember those

Chapter 3

with children wanting to get home, to kiss their partners and hug their children. Most said they had a sense of being overwhelmed by the sheer numbers of dead involved; a sense that, in spite of the work they had done, it was only a drop in the ocean.

My team leader and I sat with different counsellors and did our best to make sure they were all right before they went home. I bid the last one goodbye and told her I would see her in the morning. Now it was my turn to reflect on what had happened. I sat in the office for ten minutes or so, taking in the silence and reflecting on the enormity of what we were up against. I was well aware as I headed off into the night that we were all going to be back here tomorrow doing the same thing.

I admit that I arrived home that night and drank too much whiskey. I just wanted to numb any feeling. It worked but I knew more of the same was on the way.

My wife suggested to me that night that she would be glad to help out with the families as well. As an experienced social worker, she was brilliant with people. She would have been an ideal choice as she had experience across the board in many areas of trauma and death. But I couldn't bear the thought of her coming into contact with this scale of devastation and trauma and said I didn't need her help. I

Catastrophe on the roads

realise now, this wasn't done to protect her, but to selfishly protect me. I needed someone outside to be there for me, someone external who was untouched by it all. I needed to do this without her but I wanted her to be there for me too. To be honest, I think that accepting her offer might have been a good thing because she would have done a magnificent job. The decision though, was made for selfish personal reasons. Now, at a great distance, I can make sense of my actions at the time.

While I was supporting other counsellors, I thought I had no need for support. I was someone who was made for this work. I was rarely affected by the death that was happening around me. I would deal with a specific situation and then go home. I felt as though I could and did leave work at work. But something wasn't right this time. I could sense it. The Grafton bus crash in its enormity was overwhelming. It was the first time I had felt this way and I was determined to overcome any emotions that arose. That first night, my wife Helen sat with me and we spoke a little about what had happened during the course of the day. Well, I did the speaking and she listened. I didn't realise how long I had been talking until I looked at my watch. I had been talking non-stop for nearly half an hour. I needed a good listener that night. Thankfully, I had one.

Chapter 3

The following day went the same as the first; social workers meeting family members providing details of their dead relative, morgue staff, doctors and police officers all working together to identify the dead.

Family members would go into the viewing area and see the bodies of their loved ones. It was an emotional time, a painful time. We had to cover parts of the dead with blankets and sheets as many of the injuries were horrific. People were literally in pieces from the truck that tore through the sleeping passengers on the bus. The family members of two young girls who had died spoke with each other and supported one another. The day went like the first but with less panic; we now knew exactly what had to be done.

Little was said. People just got on with the job. They were tired and beginning to fray at the edges a little. It appeared at times to be never ending. I still can't believe it, but the process was finalised late on that second day. All people had been identified. All family members were told that an autopsy would occur. I questioned the need to conduct autopsies on the victims. Wasn't this an added insult to the families as it was pretty obvious why they had died?

'No,' said the coroner. 'We need to do autopsies as testing will show things that the naked eye cannot. The autopsies might find things such as high concentrations of carbon

Catastrophe on the roads

monoxide in the blood, possibly indicating a leak in the exhaust system. This could then potentially be the cause of the collision.'

As it turned out, the autopsy found that the driver of the truck, who died in the crash, had an exceedingly high concentration of a stimulant in his blood to help keep him awake while driving long distances, a stimulant similar in effect to the amphetamines. Concentration of the drug, ephedrine, was 80 times higher than the normal therapeutic level. The consequences of the coronial inquiry saw legislative changes that banned drugs to keep drivers awake, such as ephedrine, and mandating regular rest periods for long-haul drivers.

Thankfully for the families, the autopsies were done quickly so the dead could be released to their families. At the same time, my colleague and I were trying to work out follow-up counselling for the families of the victims. I'm not sure how successful this was as there were very few public services available for people requiring bereavement care. We wrote a series of letters to community health centres but I'm not certain as to how the families fared. We couldn't do it ourselves. There were just too many.

In retrospect, and with the benefit of experience, I would have done some things differently, particularly for

Chapter 3

the bereaved. I feel we probably let down a great many people. I now know that these people would have benefited from follow-up bereavement counselling but this requires proactivity. In other words, you have to reach out to people, to offer help rather than waiting for people to contact you. Don't expect many calls from the bereaved. Often, the bereaved can't get out of bed, let alone pick up the phone to ask for help. My time at the morgue taught me this. Be proactive. Make the call. Don't wait for people to call because most times, they won't. This is something that I have taken with me and something we can all learn from. Sometimes people want help but don't know how to ask or who to ask. We can make the offer. Of all the thousands of calls I made over the years, I have never had anyone object to being contacted. Some people might thank me for the call and leave it at that, but no one ever objected. While some bereavement services still rely on clients making the call, I feel that it just shows a lack of understanding of the bereaved and their needs. Sudden, unexpected, traumatic deaths cause enormous psychological distress for those left behind. I really believe that by reaching out, you cause no harm. By not doing so, you are asking the traumatised bereaved to cope on their own, to fend for themselves.

That first bus crash taught the team some valuable lessons.

Catastrophe on the roads

The second bus crash taught us even more about how to cope and deal with such disasters. The second crash happened on 22 December that same year, 1989, at around 2.40 in the morning. It was the height of the holiday season, three days to Christmas Day, with many of those in the buses travelling home to be with family and friends.

Two buses travelling in different directions collided head on resulting in 35 dead and many others severely injured. It happened near Kempsey in the north of New South Wales. This time, the injuries were different. Buses travelling at speeds of around one hundred kilometres per hour came together with a huge amount of force. Seats were ripped from their anchor points throwing the seats and their occupants forward in a giant concertina movement. Crush injuries, especially around the chest and pelvic regions were common. There was less tearing of human tissue this time but the injuries inflicted on the victims were no less confronting. I received the call early. 'We have another one.'

We were not expecting the enormity of the first crash, let alone a second one of even larger proportions and within such a short time span of each other.

I was initially told that all had perished; the crash and subsequent injuries were so severe. Be prepared for two busloads of dead bodies. I thought at the time that would

Chapter 3

be about 80 people. I was terrified at that prospect. We had just worked on a crash involving twenty-two people. What were we going to do with eighty? Still, maybe they got the number wrong. I decided to wait until those at the accident scene had produced their report.

I immediately made calls to the hospital senior social workers who had helped last time. They all agreed they would do what they could and provide counsellors or they would come themselves. I heard later that day that about thirty-five people had died. Police and ambulance workers were on scene and we would receive the dead the following day. The same men and women gathered at the morgue for a briefing later that day. Each person was allocated a team and went home to rest before the onslaught of the next day. I arrived early, anxious to be there for the team of counsellors. Others arrived in small groups, holding cups of takeaway coffee.

'I haven't had a smoke since the last crash, John. What are you doing to me?' one of the counsellors joked. She promptly turned and began to walk outside for a cigarette.

'Did you at least buy some this time?' I shouted at her back as she left the room. She turned and smiled at me. 'Yes, I bought two packs, for the others as well.' With that, she disappeared outside.

Catastrophe on the roads

The day was long. We were anxious to try to get the work done quickly so we could release the bodies back to their families. I spoke with the counsellors at the end of the day, again to make sure they were not too traumatised.

'How did you go today?' I quizzed one social worker.

'You know I did ok. I think I was more prepared this time. I think I knew what to do and where to go more than the first time. You know it sounds weird, but I enjoyed myself this time. Last time I was just scared. This time, well, I felt more comfortable. Does that sound weird to you? Maybe I'm just a nut who likes this sort of work. Maybe I'm sort of cut out for this type of work. Yea, I know I'm strange.'

I wasn't surprised by the comment. I said, 'No, not all. Far from it. People like yourself are made for this work. There are people who can work under extreme pressure and still be human and work with people in a really genuine way. You know one thing I've noticed since these two tragedies happened. I see people judging themselves to see how well or how badly they've done. In their own minds, they assess whether they've done a good job or not. If they think they've done a good job, they are happier and less prone to being affected by the nature of the disaster. I think that's true for you. You are happier with the job you've done and so less affected by the carnage around you. You also stuck to your

Chapter 3

own task and didn't get distracted. That's always a good sign. You should be happy. From what I saw, you did a great job. Thank you so much for all your efforts. I really appreciate it.'

She smiled. 'Maybe that's true. Still I'm really pleased you asked me and I'm happy that I could help. I really feel sorry for the families I saw today. It's just all so sudden and traumatic for them'. She looked down at the floor. 'Some of us are going for a drink. Do you want to come too? I think it might get a bit messy.'

'No, I can't. I've still got stuff to do and besides I want to get home sometime as well.'

I took a valuable lesson from that interaction. I realised how true it is that people seem less affected when they think they have done a good job. When they judge that their efforts are a relative success, they seem less prone to suffering psychological issues later on. I passed that lesson on to others over the years, and most seem to agree. Most of the counsellors I spoke to after they had finished their work said similar things. They were grateful to have been given the opportunity and were pleased to have helped.

I am struck to this day by their generosity of spirit and their kindness. We managed to formally identify the dead during the course of the week and most were released to their families. I was asked by the director to check on the

Catastrophe on the roads

staff, to see if they were ok. I spoke with some of the doctors and some of the assistants. Most of them said they were fine, that this was a job they chose to do. I got the sense that some of this was bravado, a show to demonstrate they could cope with anything. That was very much the culture at the morgue. You learned to keep your emotions in check. I was never asked how I was coping. It was just accepted that I would. Doing the work on a daily basis helped me deal with the horrific tragedies of those few months. I think all of us who worked on those crashes developed high-level skills, experience and the ability to deal with death on a large scale. But sometimes things are not as they appear, even to ourselves.

I thought that I could handle most things thrown at me. I didn't realise that the work was slowly and gradually changing me. I didn't realise that until much later. It was like a slow-acting toxin, ever so gradually infiltrating my being, making slight but marked changes to the way I viewed the world, the way I acted and interacted with people around me. I was only six months into the job.

I think I know why these events touched me in such a profound way. They were not part of the normal routine at the morgue. None of us were accustomed to dealing with dead bodies on such a scale. Yes, we dealt with sudden death all

Chapter 3

the time, day and night. The sheer scale of the two disasters – the number of dead and the horrific state of the bodies – was difficult to come to terms with. So many people dying in one instance, it tested our ability to coping with death in large numbers.

There were more disasters after these two tragedies. Many of the same teams were involved in the later disasters. Some of the same team worked on a landslide when eighteen people died. This was a catastrophic landslide that happened in the ski resort of Thredbo in the Snowy Mountains on 30 July 1997 in the middle of the ski season. Two ski lodges were obliterated as one toppled into the other. As it happened at about 11.30 pm, guests were in their lodges asleep rather than on the ski slopes; unfortunately as this dramatically increased the casualty list.

Another incident that tested the endurance of staff at the morgue was the Bali bombings on 12 October 2002. The bombings took place in Kuta, a popular tourist spot in Bali. The attacks were carried out by members of Jemaah Islamiyah, a violent Islamist group, who aimed to kill or main foreign tourists. Of the 202 people who died, eighty-eight were Australians, fifty-five of which were flown to the Glebe morgue as they had lived in New South Wales.

Since these big events, there have been others, of course.

Catastrophe on the roads

But, for me, those first two bus crashes were my initiation into the mass-casualty disasters. Fifty-six people dead in total, many more injured. I remember the numbers so clearly. I remember the dead filling the mortuary tables, the horrific injuries that had been sustained. I vividly remember the pressure the team felt to expedite the disaster victim identification process. We received many calls from well-intentioned people including members of the clergy and members of parliament to hasten the job we had to perform. We had journalists contacting us to find out as any details as we would be willing to provide. The coroner stood firm and insisted we had to get the identifications correct; that was our priority. There would be no shortcuts, no attempt to hasten this grim task. We all learned from the experiences. We would function more effectively in the future as a team. We would all face more mass-casualty disasters in the future. The experience we gained from working on those two bus crashes would forever be ingrained in our minds and in our hearts.

CHAPTER 4

TWO SIDES OF GUILT: A SUICIDE AND A POOL DROWNING

I did a number of jobs where guilt and responsibility were the standout emotions of the loved ones left behind.

There is no best way to cope with the loss of someone when they die. Even when the person is very elderly, it is still traumatic and causes enormous feelings of loss. You still miss loved ones, no matter if they die when they're one hundred years old or twenty. Still, often it is much more devastating when the death is not expected, sudden or violent.

I've worked with thousands of people over the course of my time within the forensic environment; parents, sons

Chapter 4

and daughters, husbands and wives, lovers, partners and everyone in between. Everyone was different in the way they reacted to the loss but there were some deaths that caused the loved ones to question the part they may have played in the death. Some people felt guilt ridden. I found this particularly true in deaths due to suicide and in parents of children where they felt that their duty to protect their child had been breached.

I was involved in many counselling sessions with such people. One involved a son's suicide and the pain and guilt that the mother felt, the other was the result of a swimming pool drowning where the mother felt as though she had failed to supervise her child properly.

Joanna's story
Suicide is a very difficult death for those who have to deal with a loved one dying this way. I feel there are two different types of suicide generally – one that is instinctive, without real thought, the second a considered choice. The former often applies to younger suicides, people aged between sixteen and thirty or so, the latter applies to the more mature suicides. These people are generally in their forties and older. At work, we had to examine suicides that were reported to the coroner. The most common means

Two sides of guilt: a suicide and a pool drowning

in those times was hanging, followed by jumping from a height. Strangely, the age of the person was immaterial; the method of death was usually one of those two.

One suicide that I remember vividly is that of a twenty-year-old university student who was caught cheating during an exam. He was asked to leave and was told that he was in serious trouble. He went home, had a conversation with his mother and hanged himself from a tree in the backyard later that evening.

I received a call one day from a friend of the mother. The friend told me that the mother wasn't coping and needed help. She told me she was worried that the mother might try to do the same thing. I thanked her for her call and told her I would call the mother immediately. I rang and she answered.

'Hi, my name is John and I'm the senior counsellor at Forensic Medicine. This is where your son came after he died, where the autopsy was done. I'm ringing for two reasons really. Firstly, I want to see how you are and secondly your friend called to say she is worried about you. Can I have a few minutes of your time please?' It was vital that I try to establish a rapport quickly or I would lose her.

'That's nice of you to call and for her to worry about me, but please don't worry. I'm fine, really I'm fine ...' Her voice

Chapter 4

slipped away.

This is not an uncommon response to my concerns. Bereaved people often say the same thing, that they are fine and please don't worry which amounts to 'leave me alone' but I wasn't having any of it.

'Maybe that's true, but I don't think you're doing all right. No one would be after a loss as profound as this. You've lost your son and that's really awful and I want to help if I can.' She started to cry, huge racking sobs down the phone. I sat and listened while she cried over the death of her son. I said nothing allowing her to cry for as long as she needed. Finally she could speak.

'I can't believe he's gone. He was always so full of life. Everyone loved him. He was my gorgeous boy and I don't know what to do now. I don't know what to do. I'm lost without him. He was my everything ...' She began to cry again, All I could do was listen and wait until she stopped again.

'I am so sorry about your son. I'm so sorry he took his own life. I would like to help and I want to invite you to come in and see me, or I can come and see you if you like. Either way is fine by me. How about I come next Tuesday at 10 or you can come here. Let's make a time now. Does 10 suit?'

Two sides of guilt: a suicide and a pool drowning

I felt it was important to make a definite time when talking to bereaved relatives. It was then a set appointment that they were more likely to attend. In many ways, the bereaved can feel that they are undeserving of help or they feel they have done something wrong in some way. By making an appointment, I was more sure the person would turn up; they would now have to cancel or simply be a 'no show'. Making a definite time also said 'I care'. She agreed to meet with me the following week at her home. I parked outside a very nice looking two-story house in a very nice part of town.

'Hi, I'm John,' I offered as she opened the door. 'Thank you for coming to see me, John, but really, there's no need. I'm sure I'm fine.' She smiled wanly.

She was a petite woman, late forties, dressed in jeans and a jumper. She looked into my eyes and I could see the pain she felt. I could always tell by the eyes and her eyes were those of someone who had suffered a calamitous loss. They were red and she had bags under her eyes. Clearly she wasn't sleeping well.

'Umm, can I come in?'

'Oh, I am sorry. Yes please, come in,' she waved her hands indicating for me to enter. 'Where do you want to sit?' she enquired.

Chapter 4

'Wherever you like is fine by me. What about at the kitchen table?' I could see that the kitchen was full of natural light and the sun was playing on the table. We both sat down facing each other. She bowed her head as if praying to take away the pain.

'It's always hard to know where to start, isn't it? I ventured. 'Do you mind if I ask you a few questions first just so we can get started? First though, I'm John and I'm the senior forensic counsellor at Glebe.'

She smiled. 'I'm Joanna.'

'Ok, Joanna, some of the stuff we will talk about today is going to be painful and you will probably, no, you will definitely get upset, and that's ok. Firstly, I know that Jason took his own life here, didn't he? I gather he hanged himself from one of the trees here on your property. That's what the police report said.'

She turned around and gestured towards the backyard, readily visible from the wide picture windows. 'See the Jacaranda over there? That's where I found him. It was awful ...' She began to cry, tears rolling down her cheeks as she looked out the window. 'His eyes were open and his tongue was sticking out a little bit. Oh, my darling boy. I'm so sorry, I'm so sorry.'

'I'm very sorry for your loss, Joanna. It's truly awful for

Two sides of guilt: a suicide and a pool drowning

you ...' I left a small pause before proceeding gently. 'Do you mind if I take you back a little bit before he took his own life and ask you something about that day?'

'No, that's fine.' She turned around and looked at me, her eyes still damp from the tears.

'From what I understand, there were some allegations of cheating during an exam and he was sent out of the room. Is that right?'

'Yes. He told me that he had tried to cheat because he was terrified he was going to fail the exam. I'm not sure how he tried. I've got a meeting at the university later this week. I'm going to ask what happened when I see them. What a stupid thing to do. I wouldn't have cared if he failed, but cheating? You can't do that and expect to get away with it. I just wish he could have told me how scared he was but he was always such a quiet, gentle boy; so lovely and he was always so good to others. I miss him so much and I know that it's my fault he's gone. It's my fault.' She bowed her head; tears flowed.

'So can I ask what he said when he arrived home from university that day? Do you remember what he said when he first came in?'

'Yes. I was in the kitchen, just here actually cutting up some veges for dinner. I heard the front door open and was

Chapter 4

a bit surprised because I wasn't expecting him for another couple of hours. He came into the kitchen and stood just there.' She pointed to a spot in the kitchen.

'I could tell there was something wrong straightaway. He just stood there and I ask him what was wrong. He said "Mum I've fucked up." and he looked so upset. So I asked him what he meant and he said he had been kicked out of the exam because they found out he was cheating. I was shocked. "What do you mean, cheating?" I got angry at him and said, "What do you mean? What have you done?" He said, "I dunno, Mum. I got scared of failing and didn't want to let you down. I fucked up." I asked how could he do such a thing and told him he was stupid for cheating. I said he had let himself down and me and there would be trouble. I asked him what he was going to do about it and he just shrugged his shoulders. He said, "I dunno' Mum. I don't know what I'm going to do. I'm sorry, Mum." He kept saying he was sorry over and over and I just yelled at him. I yelled at him and he killed himself because I did that.'

Her voice grew angry and rose in volume as she berated herself and she clenched her fists in a physical sign of her fury at herself. 'Oh God, I did that. I may as well have killed him with my own hands.' Then she seemed to deflate. She rested her forehead on the table and wept. Her shoulders

Two sides of guilt: a suicide and a pool drowning

heaved with the sobbing and she cried until she could cry no more. I watched her for a few minutes until she became quiet and walked around to stand next to her, putting my hand on her shoulder.

'You didn't kill him,' I said gently, 'but I know you feel responsible.'

'Everyone so far has said not to blame myself. You're the only one who has told me I'm responsible.'

'No, that's not what I said. I said you feel responsible in some manner. There's a difference. You are not responsible for everything to do with his death but I can understand you feel responsible for aspects of it. Can you see the difference?'

'I'm not sure, John. What do you mean?' she sighed, her voice thick with emotion. 'I'm either to blame or I'm not. Everyone has told me it's not my fault but I feel as though it was my fault. I was the one who yelled at him and told him how much trouble he was in. I even called him stupid and I've never said that to him before. I never thought I would ever call one of my kids stupid. He wasn't stupid. He was a smart, kind gentle boy. He was lovely in so many ways. And I call him stupid. Oh God, how am I going to carry on this way? What am I going to do?'

It wasn't a question in search of an answer. It was the voice of a woman filled with despair and anguish.

Chapter 4

When someone asks these sorts of questions, they are not looking for the wisest answer, they are looking for recognition, someone to acknowledge what they're feeling and listen to them. People need to feel as though they are being heard. It is all too easy for people to tell them it is not their fault, that they could not have prevented it. People want to protect the bereaved. That is completely understandable. They are trying to save the person further pain. They can feel as though, in agreeing with the person, they will only exacerbate the anguish and pain. The truth is that nothing will take away the pain.

When you disagree with someone who expresses feelings of guilt, you are denying them the opportunity to express genuine emotion, genuine regret and the resulting emotional pain. It's like saying to someone who feels lonely that what they need to do is 'smell the roses' so they should not be lonely. But that's a direct negation of their emotions. Of course, it's not done with any ill intent. It's done with a sense of benevolence. Unfortunately, it does nothing to help the person who is expressing the pain.

'I don't know yet what we're going to do,' I said, 'but I plan on helping you now in what is a really awful time for you. We're going to spend some time together in discovering ways you can express your pain and your sorrow and look

Two sides of guilt: a suicide and a pool drowning

at the way you say you feel responsible. It's not going to be painless and I can tell you now that it will probably get worse before it gets any better. I'm sorry to say it's not going to be a quick journey for you. This will take time and effort and some days will be really bad but some days might feel just a little bit better.'

Hope is something that seems out of reach for many people recently bereaved. They are unable to see beyond anything but their own current anguish and pain. It's pointless saying to them that things will get better because things may not get better for them, or not for a very long time. They feel pain and a sense of longing so profound that it almost impossible to put into words. However, I do feel that it is right to suggest to someone like Joanne that things can slowly and gently improve for them. I would often say things such as this, that things may gradually improve over time but I wouldn't highlight too much hope in this early stage. It is vital to stay with them and allow them to express their pain in their own manner. Discovering this is sometimes the most helpful thing anyone can do.

Hamlet's words from Othello spring to mind. 'Give sorrow words; the grief that does not speak knits up the over wrought heart and bids it break.' What I wanted to do was allow Joanne to give voice to her grief so that her heart

Chapter 4

would not break completely, so that she would not break.

It is vital to allow the grief to surface and gently explore its nature, to ask the person how they are, allow them the chance to genuinely express how they are feeling and ask them about their emotions. Many people are uncomfortable listening to someone who is grieving so we often try to keep people busy, try to cheer them up in some vain hope that this will make them 'feel better'. The problem with this approach is that grief is not an illness but a strong need to express a sense of loss, of sorrow, a need to be heard and validated.

'I can't see myself feeling any better, John. I just feel like my heart is going to break. I can't believe he's gone and I keep expecting him to walk back in the door. I still can't believe it. It just seems so wrong.'

'I know it feels wrong and I know that it's really hard to believe that he has died and isn't coming back. A lot of people I have spoken to over many years have said similar things to me. They find it hard to believe that their loved one has gone. It often takes three to six months before the reality really sinks in for a lot of folk.'

'You mean that it really hasn't sunk in yet?' Joanne asked.

'I don't know. It's been what? Five weeks or so? Do you feel that it's really sunk in yet? Do you really believe in your

Two sides of guilt: a suicide and a pool drowning

own heart that he isn't coming back?'

She laid her head on the table once more and stayed there for a minute. 'I'm not sure. Can I tell you something strange? You're going to think I'm a bit strange. Actually, forget it, it's nothing really.' She seemed a little embarrassed and her voice sounded as though she slightly regretted what she had said.

'Can I guess the strange thing you were going to mention or do you want to tell me?' I whispered gently. She just sat there with her head laid on her crossed arms. She didn't answer.

'Have you had a sense of his presence, a sense of him being there close by, near you?'

She quickly raised her head from her arms and looked hard at me, her eyes fixed on mine. 'How could you know?' she exclaimed. 'How can you tell he's been here?'

'I can't tell you that he's been here, but all I know is that you said what you were going to tell me sounded strange and then you seemed to feel embarrassed. I put two and two together and had a guess that you might have had a sense of him being present near you. So, you're telling me that I'm right? Tell me what happened.'

'I was sitting on the bed late the other night, just sitting and thinking when I heard his footsteps coming down the

Chapter 4

hall. He always used to come in and say good night no matter what time of night it was. He'd come in and say '"Goodnight Mum" and we would sit and talk for a minute and then he'd go off to bed. I could never sleep properly until he was back home. The other night when I heard the footsteps, I thought he was back and I expected the door to swing open and in he would come.

So I sat there waiting for the door to open, but the door never did. I quickly went to the door to see if he was just waiting at the door but when I opened it, there was nothing. But I knew he had been there. I can tell his footsteps; he was there. I don't know, maybe he was trying to tell me something. Maybe he was coming back because he's not at peace. Maybe he came back to tell me something.' She shook her head. 'Maybe I'm just going crazy.' She looked at me. 'You don't think I'm crazy, do you?'

'No, I don't think you're crazy at all. All I know is that a lot of people have told me that they sometimes get a sense of the person being there, whether it's footsteps down the corridor or having a sense of their smell of maybe a gentle touch on their arm or a vision at the periphery of their sight. I can't tell you what this means or whether it was him or not. I really don't know what it means. All I know is that if I thought you were crazy for going through this,

Two sides of guilt: a suicide and a pool drowning

there would be a hell of a lot more crazy people out there.'
I paused to think about it before going on.

'I really think a lot of people have these experiences and I think for every person, they are very real. In fact, I think you're very normal. Can I ask you a question about this? How did the experience make you feel?'

I asked this as gently as I could because I wanted Joanne to explore the experience and the feelings it brought to the fore for her. Many might suggest a visit from beyond the grave might be either crazy or terrifying but for many who have had the experience, they often say it gave them comfort. They liked the fact that the person had come back and had a short visit. In my counselling, I want to allow people to define their own experience and explore what it means for them and their feelings about it.

'I wasn't scared, John. I felt quite relieved. I felt that he would never harm me. So I knew he was trying to give me a message. I'm not sure what that message was though. I've been trying to make sense of that, to work out why he would come back to see me. Maybe he was trying to tell me something.'

'Let's have a think about it then. Was his visit to you a message in its own right or was he trying to say something to you but was either unable or unwilling to do so? Or

Chapter 4

maybe, you were unable to understand the medium or the message. What do you think?'

'I'm not sure,' she said, 'but I think he was trying to tell me he was all right, that he was going to be fine, but I'm not sure.'

'You know I'm not sure either. I know a lot of people have told me this and you know what? They're not sure either. All I know is what they tell me. They feel a sense of comfort, a sense of relief. I don't know if you will ever know what the visit meant. But if it means you get some comfort from it, that can't be all bad, can it?'

'I guess not,' she said smiling at me.

We spoke more about 'the visitation' and about how she felt. I was there for nearly three hours. By the time we stopped talking, she looked at peace. Her face looked quite serene. She thanked me for my time.

I saw Joanna for counselling for over a year. I developed a good working relationship with her. We met initially once a fortnight and then about once a month. During this time, she spoke of her feelings of guilt about what had happened. She had felt an enormous sense of self blame. We explored the whole issue during these sessions and at the end she felt more at peace and was less likely to feel the burden of being guilty for her son's death.

Two sides of guilt: a suicide and a pool drowning

'So tell me Joanna, how are you doing at the moment? You know it's been over fifteen months since we first met? It's getting on for a year and a half now.'

'I've had a good month. I've been doing a bit more this month too. I've been out with some friends, catching up with my sisters like you said I should do.' She smiled.

After a brief pause, she continued. 'I'm doing well. I've had the odd down day but I know that's ok too. I don't feel so guilty about his death any more. I can see now that it was a whole combination of factors that lead him to take his own life and you know I can deal with that now. I really can.'

I smiled as I realised she really had come a long way from the self-blaming woman I had first met. Yes, I can understand how people feel guilty but I know that guilt is almost impossible to dissect and examine. A similar term, responsibility, can be used to far greater effect.

The term, guilt, is used to determine someone's culpability. It is used in courts around the world and is a final statement. It does little to encourage debate or discussion. You are either guilty or you are not. It seems all encompassing; guilty or not guilty. We associate it with crime and punishment. It is not the same as trying to establish the nature and circumstances of someone's death through suicide. It

Chapter 4

leaves no room to move, no time to appreciate subtlety, establish motives of human behaviour. Guilt as a term is far too simplistic to use in people's reactions and emotions surrounding their feelings of loss. I therefore chose to use another term, responsibility, one that is consistent with the overall meaning but one that has very different connotations. Whereas guilt is associated with crime, punishment and is a final statement, responsibility is more flexible and is often used in a more positive fashion. Responsibility can used to encourage people. 'Be more responsible,' says a parent. 'You've shown great responsibility,' says a boss to an employee. Responsibility can also be shared, divided into parts. Someone can be responsible for one thing, someone else responsible for another part of a project. In fact a whole exercise can be divided into a range of responsibilities.

This is how I manage the aftermath of a tragic death such as a suicide. 'I'm really glad to hear you're doing well. Nice work, Joanna.'

She smiled, a genuine happy smile, one that lit up her face. It had been a long and hard road coming to this moment, but there it was, a genuine expression of happiness.

'When I first saw you, John, I didn't think I could ever get through the pain. It was just all over me, you know what I mean? It was just everywhere. I felt so damn guilty.

Two sides of guilt: a suicide and a pool drowning

I thought that I had actually killed him; that it was all my fault. I've come a long way since then. I now know that there were so many things that surrounded his death. There were so many factors that had to be thought about and talked about. But look at me now. I'm seeing friends now and catching up with people.'

She stopped and looked at me. 'I guess I'm at peace now and I know he's at peace too. When you started talking about responsibility, I didn't quite get it. It didn't make sense to me because I felt so strongly that I was the one to blame. I was the last one he spoke to and I couldn't get around that. When we spoke about his own mental state, the university, the lack of his father's presence, his lifestyle, all had an effect on what happened. Yes, he did take his own life and I know that I have some responsibility but not all of it. Those talks we've had over the last year made more and more sense to me. You know what? I'm still his mum and I love him but I still get cranky at him sometimes, when I think about all the hurt he's put me through and his friends too. You know what I mean.'

'Yes, of course I do. Yeah, of course.'

Chapter 4

Gemma's story

Gemma was fortunate in many ways. She lived in a leafy, north shore Sydney suburb. She appeared to have a devoted loving husband and two great kids. Gemma was in her thirties, had money, went to the gym, went on lots of holidays and had a big pool in her landscaped backyard. Gemma's father was very wealthy. He owned a large company and his daughter was his pride and joy. He had bought the house for his daughter and his son-in-law whom he thought was a great bloke – a hardworking man who drank the right amount of the right beer. All was well until one late summer afternoon.

Sarah, the youngest of the children, was a bright and bubbly four year old with curly blond hair who had a passion for the pool. She loved being in the water, splashing and playing with her older brother, Josh. The pool was the focus of the back garden. Surrounded by a wooden deck, it had two access gates; one at the top on the deck, the other at the foot of a stairway near the side of the house. The gate at the foot of the stairway was not in great repair and the latch at the top possibly too easy for a young child to reach up and lift it open.

Between four and five o'clock one bright and sunny afternoon, Sarah must have managed to lift the gate latch.

Two sides of guilt: a suicide and a pool drowning

She climbed the stairs into the pool area. She looked at the pool, bent down and reached out into the inviting waters and in one slow motion, fell into the pool and dropped beneath the surface like a stone.

Contrary to what people believe, children don't often splash about when they fall in the water. They just drop beneath the surface. We know this because we have the closed circuit cameras recording of what happened to Sarah. Gemma's father, in his desire for security, had the cameras installed to protect the loves of his life. He didn't realise when they were installed that they would record his granddaughter's final moments of life.

Sarah came into the morgue later that evening. I didn't hear about the little girl's drowning until the following morning. When I read the police report, I reflected on my own experiences with kids near water. Whenever we took the kids anywhere near water, all I would do was count heads. I would sit and watch and count each of their little heads as they jumped and played in the water, whether it be a river or the beach or in a pool. I was a complete obsessive about their safety but I know I didn't pay attention all the time. It's not really possible for three or four hours straight.

My wife and I discussed the idea of putting a pool in at home but had quickly decided against the idea. I was too

Chapter 4

obsessed about the safety of the kids and we thought that we could never relax knowing the pool was there.

After reading the report, I rang the police to enquire about the family and was given a brief summary. The details were sparse but they did tell me that the mother, Gemma, was really distressed and that the whole family were trying to 'pull together'. I did find out that they had footage of the little girl coming up the stairs, standing by the pool and falling in. As I knew the coroner would want to see that footage, it was delivered that same afternoon.

A few of us sat and watched it in silence. The footage was clear. The camera angle covered the pool deck, and the last three steps of the stairs going down. The camera angle didn't show the gate at the foot of the steps. We saw the little girl come up the stairs and walk quickly to the side of the pool. She bent down, reached into the pool and fell in. None of us said anything for a few seconds. 'The pool wasn't secured, was it?' someone stated matter of factly.

'No, it wasn't,' the rest of us said in unison.

'I want the gates checked as soon as possible. See if they're compliant with the legislation,' stated the coroner. 'Get the police to organise someone to check access to the pool and see if there are access points that contravene the rules. Tell them I want it done as soon as they can. Give

Two sides of guilt: a suicide and a pool drowning

them a fortnight and I want a report. I gather there are other children in the home? Make sure they can't access that pool. I don't want a second drowning.'

We sat there and watched the footage again. One of the team left the room in tears. I rang Gemma soon after that meeting. I wondered whether she had seen the footage. A male voice answered and I asked if I could speak to Gemma. He said she was resting and couldn't talk. I explained who I was and the reason for the call.

'I'm her dad, John. She's been to the doctor and he's given her something to help her sleep. I just want her to get some rest and see how she goes later on.'

'Ok. That's fine. I can call back later. What time do you think will suit?'

'Look, I think she'll be fine. She doesn't need to speak to a counsellor. The family are all here; her husband, myself, her mum and she's got a stack of good friends. So I think she'll be fine really. Thanks for the call. We appreciate it.' I got the strong sense that the father was very protective of his daughter and that I wouldn't be able to get through for a while. But I did want to make contact with Gemma if I could.

'I will need to speak to her so I can explain to her what is happening with the coroner and the investigation. I'll call

Chapter 4

back tomorrow and try to catch her then, ok?' He sounded startled at that. 'Investigation?' he queried. 'It was an accident. She just fell into the pool. Why does the coroner want to investigate an accident? What will that prove? She's gone. Nothing will bring her back. It's pointless, surely.'

He sounded defensive and angry. His tone left me in no doubt that he was used to getting his own way. I knew he was the owner of a large company and was probably used to giving directions and orders.

'Any sudden tragic death such as this needs to be investigated by the coroner. When a child dies in this manner, the coroner is legally bound to investigate. It's not something that gives the coroner any pleasure but it is a necessity. The coroner needs to look at all the circumstances surrounding the death. You see the coroner can make a series of recommendations at the end of the investigation that may in fact prevent any recurrence of this type of tragic accident. Did you know that swimming pool fencing legislation was brought in as a result of a coroner's recommendation to the government?'

But, Gemma's father was adamant. 'What is it going to prove? A little girl is gone. My lovely little granddaughter has gone and nothing the coroner does is going to bring her back. So why carry on an investigation? Makes no sense to

Two sides of guilt: a suicide and a pool drowning

me. Can't you just say what happened? It was an accident.'
'That's not the way things work,' I explained with as much care as I could. A full investigation will be done. The police, working as agents for the coroner will take statements, do an examination of the pool and its fencing and then present their investigation to the coroner. Based on this, the coroner can either decide to dispense with a formal court process known as an inquest or have an inquest where witnesses are called and people are asked about the circumstances of the death. At the end of the inquest, the coroner determines five things – the identity, the time and the place of the death and the cause and the manner in which the death occurred. That's for the coroner to determine.'

'That will kill poor Gem. Why put her through this? It just doesn't seem right to me.' There was noise in the background. I could hear some voices. I heard a female voice asking who it was on the phone.

'It's the Coroner's office,' I heard him saying to someone.

Then I heard, 'Let me speak to them. I want to know what's happening.'

'No love, you don't need to. I'm taking care of it at the moment.'

' Daddy. Let me speak to them. I'm her mum, I need to know what is happening.' The phone went quiet almost as

Chapter 4

if someone had muted the microphone with their hand.

'Hello,' said the female voice.

'Hello, my name is John. I'm calling from the Coroner's office. Can I ask your name please?'

'I'm Gemma, Sarah's mum.'

'Hi. Gemma, I'm really terribly sorry for your loss. Can I offer my sincere condolences to you and your family? It must be a very hard time for you at the moment.'

'Thank you. So you're the coroner, are you?'

'No, I'm not. I'm the head of the Coronial Information and Support Program from the Coroner's office at Glebe. I was just ringing to see how you were and to answer any questions you may have about the whole process that the coroner goes through. I was just seeing if you had any questions and to see how you were doing. If you like, I can come out and see you at your place. We can sit and talk and I can explain what I can. Would that be all right?'

'Sure, that would be fine. Can you tell me first what is happening now? The police have been round here and had some man do a pool inspection and he seemed to be checking the pool fence. What does that mean? Is there something wrong?'

'To be honest with you, the police have been directed by the coroner to do an inspection of the pool and its

Two sides of guilt: a suicide and a pool drowning

surroundings, including the fencing to check on access to the pool. It's something that is always done when a death such as Sarah's happens. The coroner always wants to know how something like this can happen and in doing so, maybe prevent another death like Sarah's. Another part of the investigation is the autopsy performed by the forensic doctor here at Glebe. The doctor did an examination on Sarah and the initial findings are consistent with drowning. Nothing else of any significance was found. She appeared to be a very healthy little girl, well cared for and clearly much loved.'

At that stage, Gemma began to cry. I heard loud sobs down the line and I heard her father in the background asking what I had done to upset her.

'What has he said now? He can't go upsetting my daughter like this. Tell him to get off now. He's just making her distressed. Let me take the phone now, Gem.'

'No, Dad,' she said raising her voice between sobbing. 'He's not upsetting me. It's just that Sarah is gone and I don't know what to do. Sorry John. My dad is protective of me. Thanks Dad, I'll handle it. It's ok. Calm down, Dad, calm down. John, can you come and see me soon please?' I arranged a time to see her and hung up.

A day later, I walked up the driveway towards the

Chapter 4

house, a large double-story home on a large block. I knew the suburb. I'd been there numerous times and was well acquainted with the neighbourhood. One of my kids had actually been to a party two streets away. You couldn't afford to live there unless you had inherited money or had serious money yourself. I rang the bell and a large figure came to the door. The man was well over six feet tall and solidly built.

'I'm Les, Gem's father,' he said offering his hand.

'Morning, I'm John from the Coroner's office'. He stood in the doorframe and stared at me for a long couple of seconds.

'Look, I know that you're here to see Gem but can you not upset her. She's really fragile at the moment and hasn't been good since Sarah passed. So can you not say anything that could upset her? She really couldn't handle it. I'm just trying to do the best for her.'

'I realise that Les,' I said trying to reassure him. 'I know you're only trying to protect her. I'm sure she appreciates that. I can't guarantee that what we talk about isn't going to be distressing though. I can't say that. When I see people and talk to them, it's usually about something terrible that has happened. At the Coroner's office, we meet people under extremely difficult circumstances so naturally the

Two sides of guilt: a suicide and a pool drowning

conversations are going to be tough. Often, there is a lot of emotion and that's not necessarily a bad thing. Sometimes it is emotional and tears flow. That's normal.'

He still stood in the doorframe. I'm not sure whether it was deliberate or not but his stance seemed to indicate that I was the last person he wanted coming in.

'So, can I come in?' I queried.

'Uh, yes, sure. But please try not to upset her too much,' he repeated.

'Sorry Les, I can't make any promises.' He appeared reluctant to allow me entry but I went in anyway. A large entry hall greeted my arrival. Artworks adorned the walls.

'I'll just get Gem for you. I think she's upstairs.'

'No Dad, I'm here.' Gemma appeared through a door to the side of the entrance. 'Hi John, I'm Gemma.'

'Morning Gemma, nice to meet you.' She smiled, a slight smile, but a smile nonetheless.

'Where do you want to sit? Lounge room, kitchen?' she queried.

'Wherever you feel comfortable, Gemma. I don't mind really.'

Gemma showed me through to the kitchen area, a large friendly space where there was a large table at one end of the room and a large kitchen area at the other.

Chapter 4

'Please sit down, John. Can I get you anything? Water, coffee, tea maybe?'

'Nothing, I'm fine, thanks.'

She sat down opposite and looked across at me. Her eyes held that unmistakable look; the look that I've seen so many times in a mother's eyes, the look of absolute bereavement. She glanced away then cleared her throat a few times and looked at me again.

'So can you tell me what is happening now, you know with the investigation and the coroner?'

'Sure. I'll get to that in a minute if that's ok. Can I just ask how you are doing at the moment? I know it sounds like a really stupid question but I thought I'd ask anyway.'

'My family is great,' she replied. 'My husband has gone back to work now, but my dad is here all the time looking out for me. I guess I'm doing all right but I still find it hard to believe she's gone.'

Her head turned towards the window and she began to cry softly. 'And I know that I should have protected her. I should have been there and made sure she was safe. She was an angel. She was funny and she was smart too. I miss her so much. It hurts, you know physically and I know it's my fault too. I should have been there. I should have saved her from drowning. I'm her mum. I should have saved her.'

Two sides of guilt: a suicide and a pool drowning

Her voice trailed off and she turned and looked at me as if asking for help from then pain.

'I am so sorry for your loss, Gemma. It must hurt so much. As parents, we all feel the need to protect our kids and when something terrible happens, we tend to judge ourselves very harshly and see fault in our actions. We probably judge ourselves more harshly than other people ever would. I know that it hurts.'

'But it is my fault. I should have supervised her better.' As her voice raised with angst, tears began to fall down her cheeks. 'I should have saved her,' was all she could say.

'What's going on?' The voice came loud and cut the air like a knife. 'I asked you not to upset Gem and you're doing exactly what I told you not to do.' Her father had come in the room and he was angry. He loomed over the end of the kitchen table like some protective bodyguard and stared at me.

'Now you've upset her. Look what you've done. She's crying now. I'd like to ask you to leave. She doesn't need to put up with this,' he remonstrated.

'Dad, leave it will you,' Gemma shouted. 'Let me talk about it. I need to talk about it Dad. I can't keep it inside my head. I need to talk. I know you love me, Dad, but leave him alone. He's trying to help me. Let him help.'

Chapter 4

She stopped and drew several long breaths. She looked into her father's eyes. 'Please Dad. Let him be. Ok?'

Les stood there for a few seconds. He suddenly looked the age he probably was and seemed to shrink. His shoulders slumped and he looked every inch the distressed father and grandfather.

'Ok, baby. I'll be off then. I'll leave you with John. I'll be back later on this afternoon to check on you. Ok Gem?'

'Yes Dad, that would be good. See you later this afternoon.

She stood up and gave her dad a kiss on his cheek. 'I'll see you later this afternoon when Josh gets home from school. See you, Dad,' she smiled. 'Thanks again, Dad,' she said softly.

'No worries, darl. See you later.' He left and the room was in silence. 'Sorry about my dad. He's very protective of me.'

'Really? You think so,' I smiled. She laughed 'Yes, just a little bit.'

• • •

The coroner was really insistent. 'There's no way that kid could have reached the top of the gate to pull the latch. The examination came back and even if the child stood on her toes, she couldn't have reached it. You know what

Two sides of guilt: a suicide and a pool drowning

I'm saying?'

'Yes, I do,' I answered with a certain amount of dismay. I knew what this meant. It meant that the gate had either been either left open or it was faulty. Since the child couldn't reach the top of the gate to open it, it was clear that the child had either walked through an open gate or had managed to give it a slight push and open it.

Either way, there was an issue here. This usually meant that an inquest would be held to determine the manner of death. In other words, how could a child access the pool area so easily? Did this mean that there had been negligence by the supervising parent? Would there be a penalty issued due to the pool gate being faulty. This added another dimension to the work I was doing with Gemma.

'Gemma? Hi, it's John. Can I come and see you in the next few days please? I just want to catch up with you and fill you in on a few things here.' I waited for Gemma to respond. 'Good,' I said organising a time. 'Sounds great. See you then, Gemma.'

It is always best to talk to people face to face about such matters. As such, I would never tell someone over the telephone about this sort of issue unless it was absolutely urgent. The coroner had given me permission to speak to Gemma about the new results.

Chapter 4

'Look,' the coroner had said firmly, 'I don't want to charge a grieving mother with anything, let alone anything like manslaughter. See if you can find out what she knows about the gate and what the hell was wrong with it.'

So now I found myself visiting Gemma once again in her home. 'Gemma, I need to tell you something that's just been found during the investigation and I have to tell you it's pretty upsetting news.' Of course, she looked very concerned.

'What is it? What have they found? Is something wrong?' She fired the questions as quickly as you might expect when faced with something like this.

'Let me explain as best I can,' I began. 'When the police and their pool expert came around to your place, they did a series of measurements including the height of the fences, the gate and the gate opening control at the top. We also measured Sarah. We found there was no way that Sarah could reach the gate latch to open it.'

'But I thought that's what had happened,' Gemma stammered. 'Sarah managed to open the gate.'

'Yes, so did we initially. But now it just isn't possible that she could have reached that high. So we have to look at other explanations. Either the gate was faulty and a child could push it open or the gate was left open. Either way, the

Two sides of guilt: a suicide and a pool drowning

fact remains; she couldn't reach the gate latch to open it. Just not possible. I know it's really hard to hear this, Gemma, but can you think of any way that this can be explained?'

Her face dropped. She bowed her head raised her hands to cup her forehead and rubbed her eyes with the palms of her hands. She said nothing for a while. She sat, head bowed.

'I think it was me, but I'm not sure,' she whispered. She began to sob quietly. 'Oh God, it was me. I was hoping I was wrong but it must have been me. It must have been me.'

Her voice rose as she cried. 'On the day she drowned, I chocked the gate open to get down the side of the house to get to the back of the filter. It was to carry some stuff down there. I only did it for a minute.' Her shoulders shook as she cried again. 'Oh, baby, I'm so sorry. I'm so sorry.'

'Gemma, you said you weren't sure. What makes you so sure now? You just told me that you weren't sure and now you start blaming yourself. Tell me. What's going through your head?'

'I think I left the gate open. I think I left it open. I'm just not sure any more. It's like I can't remember it clearly. I remember chocking the gate open and moving the stuff to the filter, but I can't remember closing it. I just can't,' she wailed.

Chapter 4

'Ok, I understand. You say you chocked the gate open and went down the side near the pool filter, then what did you do?'

'I went back inside', she said.

'Which way did you go?'

'Umm, I think I went back up the side of the house. Yes, I went up the side of the house.'

'When you walked through the gate, do you remember whether it was open or closed?'

'I'm not sure,' she responded obviously trying to recreate the scene in her head.

'Ok, we're left with a situation where you don't remember closing it and so you either left it chocked open or you closed it, right?'

'Yes, that's right. But if I left it open, it's all my fault. It's my fault.'

I checked with the investigating police and they found no evidence of the gate being left open either deliberately or by accident. Certainly when they arrived, the gate was shut.

I informed the coroner that Gemma had blamed herself but there was nothing in the evidence to indicate that the gate was chocked open at the time of death. As most parents do however, Gemma maintained her self blame.

Two sides of guilt: a suicide and a pool drowning

We had counselling sessions that would often consist of her berating herself, calling herself the worst mother, the killer of her baby daughter.

Her husband, a compassionate and caring man became more and more concerned for her welfare. He rang me regularly to let me know how she was doing. I knew only too well how she was doing and I feared she may take her own life unless things turned around quickly.

'Ok. I need to talk to you about responsibility,' I said to Gemma at our next meeting. 'We've spent more than six sessions where you call yourself every name under the sun and blame yourself for Sarah's death. We will never know how the gate was opened and how Sarah accessed the pool. There are just some things we can't get answers for. I can't help there. You can't remember but you're more than willing to take responsibility for her death. Tell me if I'm wrong here.' I said this rather forcefully but I went on.

'I'm worried about you and so is your husband. We have to start getting some place here. I accept that you feel responsible for your daughter's death. I understand that you feel responsible because you think you left the gate open. But, please understand that more people than you might share the responsibility. ... No, wait,' I said as she began to interrupt. 'Just wait. Didn't you say that your husband was

Chapter 4

going to do the pool filter but he never got around to doing it? Isn't that what you said? I asked. She sat there silently taking in my words.

'Didn't you also say your dad was coming to pick Sarah up to take her to preschool but got caught up? You said that didn't you? There were a number of factors at play here, not just you but your husband and your father as well. Can you see that?'

She looked at me quite stunned by what I had said. She said nothing for a few seconds as if digesting the news I had given her. Her brow was furrowed as she looked at me with questioning eyes.

'Yes, I get that. But aren't I more responsible than them? I mean I was the one who left the gate open. No one else did.'

'You may have left the gate open, that's true. But let's work out some figures of responsibility. What I mean is that we're going to sit down and work out the relative responsibility of each person and look at other circumstances here. Here's how it works. Let's assume that responsibility in total is 100 per cent. Before we start with you, let's look at your husband. What percentage would you give him? He said he was going to do the filter and you ended up doing it instead. What's that worth? 10? 15? 20? 25? What do you think?'

Two sides of guilt: a suicide and a pool drowning

'Umm, I don't know. Maybe five per cent'
'Really, five per cent? That doesn't seem much to me. He did have a long time in which to look at the filter. Still if that's what ...'
'No wait, I think 15, no 20 per cent. He should have done that sooner. I was always asking him to get that thing fixed and he just didn't. Yes, 20 per cent.'
And so we began to explore the nature of her feelings of responsibility whilst keeping in mind that she didn't live in a vacuum and there were other mitigating factors as well. It didn't really matter what percentage she decided upon. It was a case of taking her from a place of complete self blame and guilt to one of shared responsibility. If she could recognise this, Gemma could more easily deal with her feelings of responsibility because she was no longer alone. She felt that she was not the only one who had some share in the tragic death of little Sarah.

She had arguments with her husband over the fact he had not fixed the pool filter and she also spoke to her dad about being delayed to collect Sarah. The arguments did hurt but it also allowed the family to discuss the death of Sarah and allow feelings to be discussed that had previously been ignored completely.

There were some angry words spoken and tears shed but

Chapter 4

the family appeared to cope far better with emotions on display than the silence that had become the norm after Sarah's death. The two men central to Gemma's life did not know what to say when the little girl drowned. They kept silent not wishing to raise the questions about responsibility as they feared for Gemma and her reaction. They felt that if these things were raised, it would do harm to her. I explained to them both that nothing could hurt Gemma more than she had already been hurt. The father had lost a child and Gemma's father, a granddaughter. Nothing can hurt more than that.

The last time I spoke to Gemma, she was doing well. She had started to do some work and was enjoying getting out and living in her own way.

One of the things people ask me is how people 'get over' something like this. Others ask how people cope, others still how do you learn to live with something like this. Bereaved parents tell me you never get over it. Wrong choice of words. They also say that they can sometimes cope and, at other times, they can't. The bereaved often have told me they sometimes live with it and at other times, living seems unbearable. Losing a child is awful. Parents feel responsible when they lose a child. They have a sense that somehow they have failed in their duty to protect their child no

Two sides of guilt: a suicide and a pool drowning

matter how old, no matter how they died. What can help is developing a sense of responsibility that can be shared and explored not left to fester in the form of acrimonious doubt, guilt and self loathing.

Pool drownings are shocking. It is why governments around Australia have introduced pool safety standards such as fencing with special door closing mechanisms that are difficult for children to reach and open. The New South Wales Office of Local Government is responsible for pool safety requirements in the state. Pool owners can access the information on their legal responsibilities in regard to pool safety by contacting their local council or the Office of Local Government (or equivalent in other states).

CHAPTER 5

THESE FOOLISH THINGS ... MY WORST MISTAKE

I did a job once where I made a terrible mistake.

At times while working at the New South Wales Coroner's Court, I felt that I could cope with anything that was thrown at me. No matter how bad the death was, our team of forensic counsellors could handle it and we could handle it well. The team had been together for some time. We worked hard and became a very tight-knit unit. One of the team's unwritten rules was that laughter was allowed, even encouraged. There was very little that was off limits. The only unwritten rule was that no one ever made light of a child's death. No smart arse comments were allowed. Some of us had young children and a number of the staff within the building had kids as well. It was a rule that was

Chapter 5

strictly followed. It was never broken. However, a number of deaths were the subject of laughter and pointed remarks.

In retrospect, there was perhaps too much laughter. The laughter led to a distancing effect. Maybe that was necessary. Maybe it helped the team cope with the nature of sudden death on a daily basis. The term, black humour, is often used and I have seen it in hospitals as well. Nurses, doctors, and pretty much all health professionals have often been described as having a black sense of humour – part of their coping mechanism. Naturally, it is not shown around patients and their families but it is there, a presence in the background waiting to surface without notice. I was one of the keen protagonists of humour in the team and was ably assisted by some of the funniest people I have ever worked with or met for that matter. I'm not saying for one minute that I was following someone else's example here. I took the lead and many others followed. What had started out as nervous laughter in my first year soon developed into full-blown humour and spontaneous laughter. Very little was off limits except the death of children. We laughed when we could have cried and we laughed when we should have kept quiet.

A young woman hanged herself. She was wearing a leather bondage outfit. Whether she died deliberately or died from accidental asphyxia, I'm not certain, but she

These foolish things ... my worst mistake

died nonetheless. She was found in her home, hanging. Sadly, she had not been found for some time, and nature had begun to take its course. She was badly decomposed when she was found. Her skin had turned a muddy shade of green, her tongue was protruding, her eyes had begun to bulge. Her face was distended and bloated. In truth, she was grotesque. Decomposition is horrendous to witness.

When the body ceases to function, it starts to decay and, depending on the temperature in the room, this process can be slow or quite quick. In summer, a body can decompose much quicker than in a cold room. Either way, the body decomposes whether it is refrigerated or not. Refrigeration just slows down the process. We all know that organic foods will decay even in our home fridge. It's the same for the human body. It decays and gradually the wonder that is a human being becomes a bloated, discoloured version of its former self. Greenish marbling takes place across the body and the smell is something that is unforgettable. Generally, autopsies on decomposed bodies are performed in a separate room because the smell is often gut wrenching even though many of the assistants and forensic pathologists are accustomed to it.

Suffice to say that this young woman had died and was in a decomposed state when she was found. I had

Chapter 5

the photographs on my desk and went through each one quickly. We often saw death scene photographs. They were very much a part of the work we did. Many family members want to see photos of the deceased, where they died and so on. It might have been in a car crash, a suicide, sometimes a murder.

It was customary to always get permission from the coroner before approving such requests. Family members were always informed they could only look at photographs in the company of a forensic counsellor. If a request were made, we would then look at the photographs and contact the family to arrange a time to see them. In hindsight, this may have had an impact on those who worked in the coronial system. We would get many calls from families asking for permission to look at the photographs taken by police photographers. In fact, barely a week went by without someone making this request.

Some may ask what possible benefit a relative might gain from seeing photographs like the ones we show families. Why would anyone want to subject themselves to such a terrible ordeal of their loved one lying dead in a vehicle or surrounded by blood with visible injuries? Before I worked in forensics, I would probably have thought it would be really traumatic and be of no help whatsoever but, as it turns out, I

These foolish things ... my worst mistake

was mistaken. In many ways, it is like conducting a viewing of a dead person. The important part is the preparation before the photos are shown. I always explain exactly what is in the image before showing it to family members.

'In this next photograph, you will see him from the front. You will see he is hanging from the rope attached to the tree. He is looking down away from the camera. He is wearing a blue jumper and a pair of dark coloured pants. He has some marks on the front of his jumper that could be from some liquid dripping from his mouth. It's hard to know just from the photo. The photo is taken from the ground so we are looking slightly upwards. His face is only slightly visible from the angle of the shot. Do you want to have a look now? If at any stage you want to say no or you've had enough, please let me know. You make the decision, no one else. So, are you ready?'

And so it would go on. I would detail the photographs as best I could before showing them one by one. The benefits? When people lose someone close to them suddenly and tragically, they can sometimes feel as though they have lost control. Everything has been taken away, and they feel as though people are often telling them what they can and cannot do. They feel as though their right as a loved one or next of kin has been taken from them and it is important

Chapter 5

they are allowed to regain some sense of control.

By allowing them access to photographs, they are being given the opportunity to make decisions as to what is best in their own interests. Rather than someone saying that they can't do this or that, they at least can make some decisions about a part of the process.

Despite the fact the photographs may be confronting, I found that people were grateful to be able to access them. Some have said that their imagination of what happened was much worse than the actual images. That is the second point. People have imaginations. Often their imagination can paint a worst-case scenario that is nothing like the reality. Showing them the reality can help them understand the nature of the death, the intricacies and the facts. When you give people the facts, they generally can begin to understand what actually happened.

I remember a mother of a murdered girl telling me that without the facts, without the truth, she felt she would not be able to carry on with her life. Police need the facts to solve cases. Families need facts to help them deal with the situation and get on with their lives. In some situations, it is tempting to deny access to the photographs because of a wish to protect the people from pain. I don't believe there is any benefit from this if we allow proper preparation and

These foolish things ... my worst mistake

choice – even when the body is severely mutilated. When I first arrived at the morgue, the photographs were those taken by the police photographers. Later in my tenure, we began to face another issue in relation to photographs – and sometimes video – of the deceased taken on mobile phones by bystanders and others. The photographs and footage can often be disseminated widely on social media websites. Indeed, some people would even record their own deaths by mobile phone.

I remember one case where a young man had put his mobile on a fence and recorded his own hanging. I wasn't asked by any family member to see that footage. I'm not sure what I would have done at such a request. Is it different from still images? I think, yes. The video footage is much more graphic somehow, showing the last minutes of someone's life. The movement of life followed by the stillness of death is so profound that it is enormously powerful. To witness the death of a family member on video would be an extraordinarily disturbing experience, especially if the death had been violent and unnatural. Would it be too painful? Would it be overwhelmingly traumatic? How would one deal with seeing such video images? How would next of kin or other members of the family respond? Would it be too much for people to comprehend? I pose the questions not to come

Chapter 5

up with a definitive answer, but because these questions need to be considered in a world where mobile phone images and video can be posted on social media for all to see.

Another source of images is CCTV footage. Occasionally, forensic pathologists received videos from the police. Sometimes it is because CCTV footage has captured something that helps the police to find answers to an accidental death or a murder. Such footage is common these days. There are numerous cameras throughout cities, at train stations, in shops. In short, their presence records images they were not designed to capture. From pedestrian deaths, to railway suicides, much is captured by the presence of these cameras. Yet, such footage can be a major element in numerous investigations and help coroners to determine the cause of death.

Sometimes the police bring in other forms of photographic or video evidence including those obtained from computer hard drives. In such instances, the pathologists would form a view as to the legitimacy using their forensic knowledge. They understand bullet entry wounds, injury patterns and the like and can make comment about the authenticity or otherwise of imagery. So the types of images that come into the morgue that we could show to family members has become a broad field indeed.

These foolish things ... my worst mistake

So how does all this relate to 'my terrible mistake'? The combination of black humour, photographs of dead people and the relative merits of family members wishing to see them all came to a head one day.

I received a message that a sister of the girl who had hanged herself wanted to come in and look at the photographs. As usual, I found the file and started to look through the photos. The images were of the girl hanging in her own home. This is the same girl who was wearing bondage leathers when she died and, because of the delays in finding her, was badly decomposed. All this meant that the girl was barely recognisable from the other images in the file of a very pretty young woman. I can't remember what I felt at the time but I had become immune to most of these scenes and was thumbing through the before and after photographs when one of my colleagues came in.

'So what are you up to?' he said.

'Just going through a file. The sister wants to come in and take a look at these.' I handed the photos to my colleague.

'Holy shit. She looks shocking. Does the sister really want to see those? Good luck with that. Rather you than me.'

I went through the photos again and found the contact number for the sister in the file. I dialled the number and it went to voicemail.

Chapter 5

'Hello, this is John from the Coroner's office. I'm ringing in relation to your request to see the file of your sister's death and to talk to you about accessing the photographs of your sister. This is my number and I'm ringing at about two on Tuesday afternoon.'

Just then, my colleague wandered in again and was about to say something but I put my hand up in a gesture that said to keep quiet. I finished saying what I wanted to leave as a message and, I thought, I had pressed the button to finish the call.

For some reason, I had begun to use the hands-free option on the telephone and pressing the button was all I needed to do rather than put down the receiver. I turned to my colleague and explained that I was just making a call to the sister of the hanged woman.

'I hope she's not as goggle eyed as her sister is,' I said. What I thought was an off-hand comment induced raucous laughter from my colleague. We weren't laughing for very long, but when he left the room, I thought I heard a slight click. I wasn't sure and didn't think much about it until a short time later.

Before too long, the telephone on my desk rang and I introduced myself. A female voice said she was the woman I had just called about accessing the photographs of her sister

These foolish things ... my worst mistake

who had hanged herself. She went straight to the point.

'I heard what you said. You obviously thought you had hung up but you hadn't and I heard what you said about me and my sister. I can't come in now and see you. There is no way I would want to speak to you about anything after what you said.'

'I am so sorry. I am really sorry for my stupid callous mistake,' I stammered. I was in absolute shock and overwhelmed with remorse that I had been so stupid and thoughtless. Someone who was supposed to be helping and assisting the bereaved relations – me – had caused enormous grief to a completely innocent woman and brought an extra dimension of trauma and sadness to her already tragic situation. She went on.

'I know that it must be hard to cope in your environment and maybe you people think this is funny and you laugh about it, but there is no way I'm going to come and see you. I am really sad to hear you speak in such a manner. Good bye.'

I'm not certain as to whether she had heard us laughing, but it didn't matter. What she did hear, what I had said, was already hurtful enough.

What I am sure about is that she was decent, polite and forthright; completely at odds with my callous and hurtful comments – even if I hadn't expected her to hear them. She was reasonable and even understanding of the situation

Chapter 5

and she had insight into how we learn to cope dealing with the dead and their families. I had nothing to hide behind. It was my fault. I had made a shocking and unforgivable error of judgement. I had hurt someone badly through thoughtlessness and callousness. I sat there in silence for a few minutes.

My thoughts whirled through my mind. She had the proof of my unprofessional conduct and she could make a complaint against me. I was on tape. The hurtful things I had said were on tape. I kept thinking how could I be so thoughtless? What have I become to hurt someone so badly? Am I that immune to this work that I have lost any sense of decency? I was never worried about a potential complaint. I deserved that and more. I was more concerned about my behaviour. What had I become? Was life so meaningless now that it had all become a joke to me? I was shattered. I could not believe what I had done.

'So how did it go?' came a cheerful voice as my colleague wandered in. Seeing my face the tone changed. 'What's wrong?'

I told him what I had done, that my comment was taped, that the phone was working after I thought I had hung up the call. 'Oh shit,' came the reply.

'What have I done? I can't believe I've done that. I've just

These foolish things ... my worst mistake

become so much of a smart arse; I can't help myself. I don't care if she complains. I'd deserve that too. I just really hurt her and she was really decent. She actually understood some of the reasons why I said it. Can you believe that? She actually was really decent. Here's me being an absolute prick and she is being understanding. Shit! I'm going to get Joanna to call her and speak to her. At least she can see how she is and see if she can help.' Joanna also worked as a counsellor and she was a very good one.

I explained the situation to Joanna detailing what I had done and she looked very disapproving. I could understand that.

'John, you have to be more careful and stop saying those stupid things,' Joanna rightly reprimanded me. 'You're better than that. You don't need to say those things. It's not you.'

'Well, it clearly is. I've stuffed up and I'm asking you to speak to her as soon as you can. I know what you're saying Jo. I don't quite understand it myself. I am so sorry for her. I just feel like shit.'

'So you should, so you should,' Joanna agreed.

Joanna came back shortly after to let me what had transpired. Jo was a passionate advocate for the bereaved and never had a bad word to say about anyone. She was a woman who had been a teacher and was desperate to help people as

Chapter 5

best she could. I was grateful to have her as a colleague.

'She's a remarkable woman,' she started. 'She's not going to make a complaint but she is deeply hurt. What you said really hurt her. She doesn't want any further contact with us but she has my number if she changes her mind. I've left it up to her to contact me if she wants. John, that was really stupid,' she said sternly, stating the obvious.

'I know and I understand. I feel like shit for putting her through this. I just wish I could turn back the clock and … you know what I mean.'

'I explained to her that you are not like that and that this was a just a stupid mistake.'

'Thanks. I appreciate that. I just feel terrible for her.'

'So you should,' she repeated. 'So you should.'

I'd spent much of the decade prior to this incident caring for families and individuals as much as I could. I was genuine in my desire to help families through tragic and traumatic events. Maybe this was some sort of sign that my work was getting to me. Maybe I had run out of empathy. Maybe I had stopped caring. Maybe this was the end.

The incident stuck in my mind and has never been far from it, even years later. Of course, I never used hands-free when calling again. And I stopped making the smart comments to my colleagues, before or after any calls or meetings with

These foolish things ... my worst mistake

family members. I was always far more vigilant and careful about how I said things, how I interacted and how I spoke.

Part of me was never the same again. I didn't see things in quite the same light any more. While I am some distance now from what happened, I still deeply regret what I said on that day all those years ago. I wish I could take back the hurt I caused that woman. I wish I could make it up to her in some way. But, I know I can't. I just fucked up.

CHAPTER 6

AFTER HOURS AT CRIME SCENES

I did some jobs once where I was called out to the places where deaths had taken place. I soothed, I nurtured and even once, I fought back.

We had an on-call system for counselling at Glebe. This means that a counsellor would be available for counselling family members or witnesses any time of the day or night. We carried a pager because in those days mobile phones were not readily available and coverage was limited. We would carry the pager – about the size of a modern mobile phone – and if we were needed, a message would be sent to the pager to alert us that we were required at the morgue to provide support. It was always due to a sudden death from various situations – from a house fire, a car accident or a

Chapter 6

suicide. It varied from week to week.

When I first started working at the morgue, pager calls were minimal. No one really knew of our existence and so call outs were quite rare. As time went on, the police and the mortuary assistants became quite accustomed to contacting us to support the bereaved soon after the death. This usually meant we would attend one of the two mortuaries and perform a viewing of a deceased person. Families would attend the morgue to say goodbye to the person who had died. We would offer support and guidance to those attending the viewing. It became commonplace that we would be 'paged' to come in when not on duty. It gradually became rare not to be called in over the weekend. Sometimes, we would be called three to four times to conduct viewings or assist the police in performing more distressing identifications on bodies that had undergone significant trauma.

The police would be concerned as to someone's ability to cope with the distressing news and would call us to help a person or make an assessment as to their support needs. We would generally hold the pager for a week and then hand it on to another team member. The after hours work was probably even more challenging than during the day as there was less support for the team member on the weekends or

After hours at crime scenes

late in the evening.

When the pager went off at night, I always followed a ritual. I would check on the kids before I left the house. I would look in at the kids in their cots or beds and make sure they were breathing. If they were still, I would give them a slight shove to get them to move. The kids would generally move a little or make a small noise and then settle again. I told this to a number of police and fire officers. Many seemed to share a similar ritual. I guess we wanted to reassure ourselves that our kids were safe and this little ritual seemed to provide some degree of comfort for us.

As time went on, the police began to call us out to the scene where a death had occurred. I'm not certain as to how this happened initially but I gradually got called out to more and more locations.

Attending a home where someone had died was a very different experience for me. The clinical environment of the morgue meant you could more easily distance yourself from the death. It is easier to make it all a little bit more removed from our own lives. But when entering someone's home, there is a greater sense of who the person was, how they lived their lives; their loves, their hobbies and interests.

I walked down many hallways and saw pictures of the dead person with their family, their husbands or wives, happy

Chapter 6

and smiling. Sometimes, I would recognise the location of the picture and think that's where I took the kids recently or that's where Helen and I went to dinner. It just made it all a lot more uncomfortable. I went inside a number of lounge rooms to find collections of music similar in taste to my own, a disconcerting thought. The more I was able to identify with the person, the more it brought death closer to home and reduced my ability to distance myself. Generally the jobs I attended after hours at people's homes were ones that were distressing for all. Cases of house fires where kids were burnt to death, cases where a mother went seemingly mad and killed her own child, or a suicide where the person was still in the same position as when they had died. It was raw and sometimes very emotional.

The attending police and ambulance personnel were often upset at some of these incidents. I came to know a number of crime scene or forensic police officers. They were all highly trained and skilled officers and all, on the whole really, decent men and women. They were dedicated people and mature enough to deal with this very challenging work. I would often see them at the scene and we would speak freely about observations of the scene and their take on what had happened. Most uniformed police officers were quite young but had been given some training in working in these types of situations. They did their best when dealing with highly distressed individuals, tearful and angry family members.

However, that was my job; to deal with the families in their distressed state and to try to assist them in the best way I could manage. Sometimes family members would become highly agitated and want to see the dead person as soon as possible. At other times, I found that humour worked to diffuse a tense and emotional time.

On one occasion, I was called to a home in the south-western suburbs of Sydney. A young man had killed his father and then turned the gun on himself. The home was quite secluded set in a bushy area. It stood alone at the end of a narrow street. Arc lights were clearly visible at the beginning of the street, cutting the night air and giving a harsh atmosphere. As I drove slowly down the street I was waved down by a police officer.

'Sorry mate, the street's closed for a police operation. You'll have to turn around.'

'Yeah, I know. I was called by the sergeant in charge to come here. I'm John from Forensic, the counsellor.' I showed him my ID.

'Ok, mate, I'll just write your name down and you can go up. Just park before the lights. We're taking some photos and doing a video at the moment so just stay out of the way.'

Chapter 6

'Ok, thanks mate.' I parked down the road, just before the arc lights. They shone down on a scene that clearly showed two men on the grass lawn in the front of the property. One was wearing a singlet and shorts, the other wearing a pair of shorts and no shirt. As I approached I could see one was an older man, the other maybe in his twenties. One had a significant head injury; the other had what appeared to be chest wounds. His shirt was torn, possibly from an attempt at resuscitation.

An older police officer waved at me. 'Hey, over here. Thanks for coming out. You're the counsellor, are you?'

'Yeah, hi, I'm John Merrick.'

'Ok, well, the wife of the deceased is in the front lounge room. She's a nice old dear. Just go in and have a chat with her and use your counselling magic.'

'What's happened here?' I wanted some basic information at least.

'The young bloke is their son. Mad as a meataxe, poor bugger. He's got a hold of an old rifle and shot his father and then shot himself. It looks like he's shot his father a number of times. I'm still waiting for the doc to come out and take a look. The young bloke's got a history of being admitted to psych centres and we've known about him for a long while. Looks like he's just finally lost it. Like I said, the mother is inside.'

After hours at crime scenes

The police officer was a big man and had a big booming voice. 'Ok, just go inside and speak with the mum. She's doing it tough.'

'All right, thanks, Sarge.' I wandered off and entered the house. I introduced myself and she told me her name was Beryl. She spoke of her son and her husband. As we talked, we would occasionally hear the big booming voice of the sergeant. 'Ok, guys. We'll finish the job soon.'

A few minutes later came the sound of a motor vehicle parking outside.

'Great guys,' came the booming voice. 'The truck's here. Everyone get something to eat. You! Get me a coffee, two sugars and milk, oh and get me a ham sandwich as well, will you?' It was an order given to one of the young officers at the scene.

These catering trucks attend some major scenes to provide food and sustenance for the police officers, ambulance officers and others who need to spend time – sometimes quite a lot of time – at the scene of a death.

A short while later, after the sergeant had obviously eaten his ham sandwich and fortified himself with the coffee, he came into the lounge room.

He addressed the mother. 'We won't be much longer, love. The doc's arrived and he won't be too long. Everything all right here?'

Chapter 6

Beryl nodded and sarge left. 'He seems very nice,' she ventured.

'Yes, nice bloke, quite loud though,' I said.

A little while later the voice came again. 'Has the truck got anything sweet? I could go some chocolate biscuits.'

Beryl looked at me with raised eyebrows. 'And he has a healthy appetite too.'

'Yes, he seems to be a good eater,' I agreed smiling. I often found that humour could defuse the anguish in these situations. When people are under stress, laughter can alleviate some of the pain.

I remember being invited to a dinner one night with a group of men who had all lost children in a horrifying mass shooting. We were invited to a Japanese restaurant in Sydney. I had dreaded the thought of being at dinner with a group of recently bereaved fathers. I remember thinking that this would be one night where there would be very few laughs. I was wrong on so many counts. We all drank too much beer, became loud and raucous and ended up laughing all night.

The men told me they had thought the same. They thought that a night with a group of counsellors would be about as much fun as having a tooth removed – without anaesthetic. We gelled brilliantly and we laughed until we could laugh no more. Humour is a stress release, a universal healing and bonding experience. Sometimes however, no amount of humour was going to work at all.

• • •

There was one case when I was called to a house where a young man had cut his throat and his sister wanted to see him. Not long after the police officers and I had arrived, the sister turned up wanting to see her brother and hold him one last time. The police were still taking photographs and conducting the usual forensic assessments.

I had seen the young man lying on the floor of his room. The serrated knife he had used to cut his own throat had caused massive lacerations to his neck and he had bled significantly. The blood had pooled around his neck and on the back of his head and he had blood spatters on his shirt and on his pants. His head was at a slight angle and his eyes were open and staring. When someone cuts themselves, you often see tentative marks from initial cutting. It is almost like they are trying it before they really make it count.

There were some tentative cuts on his wrists and some cuts on his face, all in keeping with the same knife being used. I was aware that it is not the best option to let family members access the scene itself. It is best done at a viewing at the morgue because we can organise it properly so that

Chapter 6

family members have chance to say goodbye, and to kiss and caress the person.

It is very different at a scene where there is blood and obvious signs of trauma. In many ways, it is like seeing a horror film with blood everywhere. It could potentially cause the viewer to suffer incredibly strong traumatic reactions from the horrific scene that can overwhelm the grief they are suffering and can increase their suffering for a longer period of time.

Smell could also be present and this can act as a trigger for family members later to suffer traumatic reactions. This is why we encourage family members to view their loved one in a funeral home or at the morgue and not at a death scene. Additionally, it's important for the police to keep the scene from becoming contaminated.

On this night, I was sitting with the dead man's mother in the lounge room of the family home. The mother was sitting there crying when a figure suddenly burst through the door. 'I want to see my brother and I want to see him now,' the figure demanded.

The figure turned out to be the man's sister. Given that the young man had cut his own throat, I was very insistent that family members did not access the scene and I said this to the distressed woman.

After hours at crime scenes

'Look,' she shouted, 'he's my brother and I can see him. I want to see him. I need to see him. Just let me in. I won't cause any trouble. Just let me in.'

A young police officer had entered directly behind her and was standing looking at the woman and me. Her mother sat on the couch staring at her daughter.

'Oh love,' said the mum in a quiet voice. 'He's at peace now. He's in a better place. You don't want to see him like this. He's got cuts all over him. You don't want to remember him like that, do you love? Come and sit down over here with me.' She patted the couch seat alongside her. 'Just come and sit down here and John will tell us what's going to happen next.'

'No, Mum. I need to see him. Is he in the bedroom?'

She moved towards the hallway in the direction of the bedroom. The police officer immediately stood in her way. He was quick. She just about went straight into him and her arms came up as if to push him out of her way.

'Please sit down now.' My voice was strong and firm and seemed much louder because the room had been fairly quiet until now. 'Just sit down. I need to explain a few things to you. Oh, by the way, I'm John, the forensic counsellor.'

The young woman stared at me for a second. 'So are you going to try and stop me?'

Chapter 6

'No, I'm not going to try to stop you; I'm going to stop you with the help of my police friend here.' The young police officer looked slightly shaken at that. I could see that he didn't fancy having to physically restrain this woman.

'Now please, just sit down,' I continued far more gently this time. She stood there for a moment then turned away from the police officer and sat down next to her mother. Her mother embraced her immediately. The young woman began to cry, long heartfelt sobs as she leant on her mother. Her mother looked as old as anyone could look, her grief etched on her face as if it were carved there forever. She stroked her daughter's hair and soothed her with gentle words.

'It's all right, love. He's at peace now. You know how he was always so troubled. He wasn't well darling, you know that. He's at peace. He's in a better place.' The daughter's head peered from beneath her mother's arms.

'Can I see him, please?' she asked again, more softly this time.

'Yes, you can and I would really encourage that but that will have to wait until he's cleaned up and we can have you say goodbye with more dignity. He's not in a fit state to see now. Have you been told what happened?'

'A bit. Mum said he has cut himself and …' She began to cry once more.

'Yes, that's right,' I quietly agreed. 'He's cut himself in a lots of places but mostly he has cut his own neck. I'm sorry to say there is a lot of blood. The reason I don't want you to see him now is that we can clean him up and allow you to see him when he looks – it's hard to say this – but when he looks more at peace, more like he was in life, and, well, more dignified. I think that would be better for you rather than seeing him now. Do you understand?'

'Yeah, I guess so. So when can I see him? Can I see him tonight sometime?'

'I'm not sure. I'll have to check with the coroner and see if we can clean him up before the post mortem examination takes place. I'll do what I can. I promise I'll do my best to help you see him as soon as I can. Ok?'

'Ok. I'm Sophie by the way. Sorry about that. I'm his sister.'

'I kinda' figured that already. I'm John.'

This time I was able to pacify the young woman but that didn't always happen.

• • •

It was about eleven o'clock one night when my pager went off. I was asked to ring the police who had been called to a murder scene in Sydney's south. It turned out that it was the

Chapter 6

same booming voiced police sergeant.

'Hi counsellor. How are you? We've got a job here where we need your skills. A bloke's been stabbed to death by his flatmate. The dead guy's sister is here and is in a bad way. We could use your help.'

I agreed immediately and headed off into the night. Whenever I went out at night, I listened to the 'Love God' on radio. The Love God, Richard as his callers addressed him, had a great voice; deep mellow and always sounded so patient and supportive. I loved listening to the listeners ringing in to tell their stories. They would ring and request a song to be played for their absent partner. They would describe how much they missed the love of their life and ask for a particular song to be played. I always loved the ones that went something like this.

'Hello, Madge. I believe you have a special message for a special man tonight?'

'Yes, I do Richard. My partner's been away from home for a year now. I only get to see him occasionally and for hardly any time at all,' said the female voice.

'That must be hard, Madge. You must be missing him.'

'Oh, I am, Richard.'

'So he's away for work often is he?' asked the kind gentle and dulcet tones of Richard.

After hours at crime scenes

'No, Richard he's serving five years for armed robbery, which he didn't do. He was framed. He didn't do it.'

Richard rarely skipped a beat. He was on his game as always. 'That must be hard for you, Madge. Is there any message you'd like to send him while he's away, I mean, not home?'

And so it went. I loved this stuff. It was brilliantly escapist material I could have a good laugh on the way to a job.

I arrived at a small weatherboard home with police tape around the front of the house. A young police officer stood guard just in front of the tape. I noticed the front door was boarded up. Perhaps the space inside was being used as another bedroom or for some other purpose. I noticed that there were two paths running down each side of the house, the right-hand path slightly wider.

I approached the police officer and explained who I was. He took my name and lifted the tape to allow me access. He instructed me to go down the left-hand side as the main entry was through the rear of the home. I walked down the side and then around the back. I saw the police sergeant with the big voice who greeted me like an old friend.

'Oh g'day counsellor. Good to see you. Thanks for coming out. Well, we've got one dead man in the bedroom. He's been stabbed a few times. He's got some defence injuries so he's

Chapter 6

probably tried to stop the attack. It looks like the flatmate and him had an argument and the other bloke's stabbed him. The neighbours heard arguments this afternoon and into the night. The neighbour this side,' he said as he waved in the direction of the home next door, 'well, he told them to shut up. He saw them arguing when he stuck his head over the fence this evening. According to the neighbour, they had lots of arguments recently. Both big drinkers and smoked a lot of pot. It looks like the flatmate's done a runner and we are looking for him now. He won't have gone far.'

I went inside the home and spoke with the man's sister for about two hours. I explained that someone would call her tomorrow to keep her informed about what would happen at the Coroner's office. She was grateful and I headed outside to leave. I saw the sergeant deep in conversation with some people whom I thought were detectives.

The sergeant turned around as I came out. 'Thanks for coming counsellor. See you later.' All the men nodded at me. I'm not sure why but I remembered that the house had two pathways. If I chose the other path, it would save me all of twenty seconds. So I turned left and walked towards the path that led around the other side of the house. As I turned the corner, the light from the back of the house disappeared. The path was in darkness.

After hours at crime scenes

I stopped for a second to let my eyes become accustomed to the darker conditions. When I could see well enough so I began to slowly walk up the side pathway. I noticed a largish bush on the right near the fence line. It was about the same height as me but it seemed to have three large stumps. As I looked at these, a shape suddenly appeared from behind the bush. The stumps were in fact not stumps, two of the three being legs attached to a man. He lurched in a movement towards me and swore. To this day, I'm not sure what was said but it was not a greeting wrapped in affection. As he approached, he brought his right hand up and at that moment I knew he was going to punch me. He was not quick, maybe affected by drugs or alcohol. I'm not sure, but as he lurched forward, I stepped forward prepared to fight. It seemed like an eternity for his closed fist to get anywhere near me and as I moved towards him, I raised my left arm to deflect the blow. It struck on my forearm and bounced off.

The man grunted as the punch failed to hit the target, me. I had already begun my counter and I brought my right fist into the left side of his face. He cried out at that, his left arm coming up from his side to protect his face. I moved again and this time I brought my fist into his ribcage. He groaned as I hit him the second time. I noticed a movement over my right shoulder and a large shape moved past me.

Chapter 6

The large shape literally hit the man in the chest and hit him with such force he collapsed like a rag doll. The large shape had him with a tackle that would have put any footballing player to shame. It was a huge hit and the man was pretty much squashed. The large shape turned his head towards me.

'Grab the handcuffs there will you, counsellor. I'll just cuff this bloke.' He sounded a little out of breath. I stopped and stared at the scene. 'Just grab them and pass them here,' insisted the sergeant. I shook my head and grabbed the handcuffs.

'There we go,' he said as he handcuffed the man. 'I reckon you have to be the flatmate,' said the sergeant who had seemingly moved like a gazelle when he realised what was happening on the side path. I thought to myself at the time, he is a 'flat mate', especially after you squashed him. Two other police officers had arrived and half carried, half lead away the man.

'Well, that was fun,' boomed Sarge. 'You all right there, counsellor? You did well. I saw you land one on him. I thought I'd better step in. I didn't want you to have all the fun.' He smiled. 'You all right? No injuries? Good as gold, eh.'

We spoke for a while longer but I really didn't hear that

much. I was probably in shock but the cheerful and good-natured sergeant made sure I was fine before I headed off.

As I drove home, my brain was still whirring at a thousand miles an hour. I stopped near a park on the way back and sat there in silence. I had not been in a fight since high school, my last attempt being a fight with the school bully who had landed more punches but who hadn't won outright. I had studied martial arts for years while at school but I'd never actually used it. I suddenly realised some of the moves I had done tonight were from days gone by. Maybe some of it had actually stuck. I laughed to myself. Maybe I had actually learnt something. I didn't mention this to anyone but deep down, I was actually feeling quite proud. I had helped to catch a suspect in a murder case.

CHAPTER 7

HITTING THE WALL

I did a job once that saved my life.

Maybe the work I was doing was starting to take its toll. Maybe I hadn't realised that doing the things I did and the things I saw and heard, made me vulnerable in some way. To this day, I'm not sure. The most common means of suicide is hanging. Over the years, I had seen many people end their lives this way. The second highest means of suicide is to jump from a great height. The Gap, in Sydney's eastern suburbs, is a location often used by people who want to end their lives. It is a long drop to the rocks below from the cliff face. Because it is a place where people commit suicide, it is fenced off to the public but many people still manage to gain entry.

At the top of the cliff, you can see the waves crashing on the rocks beneath your feet. I'm not certain how high the

Chapter 7

cliffs are but I'm certain that when you jump, there is little chance of survival. North Head is another location that is popular among those who decided to jump from a height to their deaths. Often when people jump from The Gap, a fisherman or someone in a boat can spot their bodies floating just off the coast. Sometimes the bodies can be wedged in the rocks but usually the bodies are washed off the rocks by the strong waves.

These bodies are often severely traumatised and sometimes hard to recognise due to their faces or heads being damaged by the fall or the waves washing them out to sea. In these cases, a forensic dentist is needed to help identify the deceased. In such situations, the forensic dentist needs to obtain ante mortem records from a dentist and then match those records with their post mortem findings. Dental identification is accurate and it can be done very quickly. It also means that expensive DNA testing is not required. When someone is too damaged to identify, missing persons lists are checked and invariably we discover their possible identity very quickly. Family members or friends often contact the police to alert them to their concerns about a missing person. The treating dentist (of the dead person) would then be contacted for dental records and these would be supplied to forensic almost immediately. All this is

Hitting the wall

undertaken because the visual trauma to such bodies makes the regular visual identification impossible. I knew this. I knew this very well.

It's hard to explain how I myself started having suicidal thoughts and I still cannot understand it to this day. All I know is that I was suicidal at that time, and decided one day that I would end my life by jumping from The Gap. My body would be identified by dental means and that would spare my wife from undergoing the trauma of having to identify my body.

At the time, I got the notion into my head that my family would be better off without me. I had checked how much money would be available for my wife and the kids and thought they would probably miss me for a short time but they would move on quite soon and would be in a better situation financially. I had convinced myself that this was true. God knows why I thought that but I did. It's really difficult to explain with any clarity the reasons how I came to be in this state. I think it's a question of a reduction in choices that the person feels they are able to make. It's almost that the person is unable to see the choices available. In effect, it's a sense of blindness, an inability to see more than one potential solution.

I'd seen many suicides over the years. Whether young and

Chapter 7

old, suicide has a pattern that can be followed. Many times, the young ones take their own lives impulsively. There are many deaths that seem to occur without much thought. It is as if the person underwent some particular incident that prompted the taking of his or her life shortly after. The suicide of the young man who hanged himself after being caught cheating in a university exam is one example of this seemingly spontaneous suicidal response. Dozens of young people, particularly young men, may have had something acutely painful happen to them, such as the breakup of a relationship which prompts them to end their lives soon after.

I remember some young men throwing themselves under trains following relationship break ups which seems to be done on impulse. There may well be some long-term underlying issues but the final trigger that appears to shoot the last bullet is often something immediate and traumatic. In my experience, it seemed that youth, as ever, acts impulsively.

Suicide by older, more mature people in their late thirties and upwards appear to be more considered. These suicides appear to be planned for a period of time, at least a week and sometimes longer.

There were many times when we would find out that the

Hitting the wall

man who took his life on a Saturday had in fact bought the rope the week before from a hardware store. According to family and friends, the person who died had seemed to be a bit more happy than usual and appeared more relaxed than they had been previously. It was almost as if the decision had been reached and they were at peace. They had planned it and made sure that things were in place to ensure a degree of certainty. I realise that these are my observations only and I accept that but I feel confident that this is the case – older people are more considered and younger ones act more on impulse.

While hanging and jumping from a height are the two most common forms of suicide, throwing oneself in front of a moving train is another. It is surprising that this can happen at all given there are so many CCTV cameras on train stations. The cameras however, do allow the coroner and those of us working at the morgue to see the person before they jump. I have seen numerous videos of people who have taken their own lives by throwing themselves in front of trains. The footage also shows the person before the event and what is striking is that they appear so calm.

Often the footage shows the person walking down the stairs to the platform, not with the gait of someone about to end it all but with a relaxed gait, someone who, on the

Chapter 7

face of things, appears to be in good spirits. We would watch as the person would sit on a bench on the platform, sometimes doing something ordinary like drinking from a can of soft drink and then calmly jump in front of the train as it approaches. That surprised us all who work in forensics. We all expected to see someone who was nervous, someone who looked distressed or anxious. Far from it. These people almost seemed to have a spring in their step. Maybe they were so sure, at least in their own minds, that what they were doing was the right thing for them. Maybe that was what I felt all those years ago.

Some years prior, I worked at a major hospital in Sydney and part of my work was to speak to young people who had attempted suicide. Sometimes they had tried by cutting their wrists, sometimes by an overdose of drugs, occasionally they had been found in a car attempting carbon monoxide poisoning. They were of differing ages, some in their early twenties, some in mid- to late-teens. All had slightly different stories. Some had tales of lost love, others cited oppressive parents whom they wanted to escape, others felt they had been bullied at school or by their peer group. They told me their stories to explain why they had attempted suicide.

They cried, some wishing they had been successful, others grateful they had survived. One thing that struck me was

Hitting the wall

some of the similarities in their stories. In the days before they attempted suicide, they had considered few options were open to them. They might have had an issue with a girlfriend or boyfriend. They initially believed they had a choice, maybe the first being to speak to their boyfriend/girlfriend, secondly to seek advice or support from a friend or family member, the third option to take their own life. So, initially they had felt that they had a choice. Then later they felt their options narrowing so that they only saw one option, to take their own life. What intrigued me was that time when their options seemed to disappear, when their choices went from three to one. Why? What happened during that critical time that led them to believe that there was only one option? These young men and women had all reached the conclusion that suicide had become their only choice. I asked them to explain some of their thought processes during the week before the attempt, in order to establish their choices and then the subsequent reduction to the final option. I remember the discussion with one nineteen-year-old woman who lived to tell her story.

'Ok, you tried to end your life yesterday by taking the overdose of tablets?' I asked.

'Yes, I guess so,' came the whispered response.

This young woman had taken pills and was found by her

Chapter 7

younger sister when she arrived home from school. She had been admitted to hospital and was successfully treated. She was still a little drowsy but in good health overall when I saw her. Her parents were at the hospital as was her sister all very anxious to ensure her recovery. She was whispering because she had trouble speaking due to a sore throat.

'What made you decide to end your life yesterday as opposed to the day before? What I mean is, why yesterday?'

'I dunno,' came the sullen response. 'Maybe I thought that it just wasn't worth living anymore.'

'I didn't ask that. What I asked was what are the reasons you chose yesterday and not the day before or leave it until today. Why yesterday? Can you tell me that?'

The look on her face was one of confusion. She looked as if she didn't quite understand the question.

'All right, let's look at it another way. Can you tell me when you didn't feel you were suicidal? Two days ago, three days ago? When do you think?'

'Umm, I guess I felt ok on Saturday, no, on Sunday. Yeah, I felt ok on Sunday. I didn't think I was suicidal on Sunday. I went to a shopping centre with my sister. Is she all right? I haven't seen her yet? Is she here?' She looked towards the door.

'She's upset. She's really upset. She is the one who found

Hitting the wall

you at home. She's the one who rang the ambulance and got you here so the staff here could save your life.'

'I'm sorry I upset her. I'm really sorry.'

'Don't tell me,' I said. 'Tell her. Your Mum and Dad and your sister are outside at the moment. When we finish up here, I'll get them to come in. Are you ok with that?'

'I'm worried what they'll say. I think Mum and Dad are going to be … I don't know. Maybe relieved, maybe not. I'm not sure whether they really do …' Her voice trailed off and she was silent.

'Really do what?' I asked gently.

'Whether they really do love me.'

'I don't know if they do or not. I haven't got to know them well yet but they look as though they do based on what they have said outside. Your mum's been crying non stop and your dad looks pretty red eyed too, but maybe that doesn't mean they love you. Why else would they cry or look upset?'

'Maybe they do. Maybe they do love me. I just thought they didn't. When I told them I was leaving home, Dad and Mum got all shitty with me and told me I couldn't leave home until I got a job and started earning money. But I was ready to move in with my friends and just live on a benefit, you know get money from the Government.'

'And your mum and dad weren't pleased with that?'

Chapter 7

'That's right. They told me to stop being stupid, to get a job and start working and then they said I could move out.'

'Yes, I understand. But can I take you back a couple of steps first and talk to you about what I was talking to you a minute ago. I just want to make sure I understand something clearly. So you said Sunday was a good day with your sister and today is Wednesday, so what happened on the Monday and Tuesday? Just talk me through those days please.'

'On Monday I went and saw my friends at their new unit. They've just moved in and I went to check it out. It was really great. They had space and it was near the station. Mel's dad had paid for most of the rent and the deposit so they only have to pay a bit. They're both working and they asked me to move in. I wanted to get away from home and their place was ideal. I said yes, of course. But when I got back home I spoke to Mum and she said no way. She told me to get a job first and then Dad said the same. He said I had to get my act together and start working. He yelled at me and Mum and him had a fight afterwards. Mum said afterwards I was selfish and I was acting like a child. She told me I wasn't going to move out any time soon with my attitude. She told me to get a job or go and do some study. It's just not fair. I'll miss out on staying with my girlfriends if I don't move out soon.'

Hitting the wall

'We'll talk about that a bit later, ok? Now what happened on the Tuesday?'

'I got up after Mum and Dad had gone to work. Jess was still at home and she went to school soon after. She didn't say anything to me either except that I was a stupid bitch and then walked out.'

'Ok, then what did you do?'

'I was real upset and I decided that I was going to do something. I was going to move out to the girls' place. They would have me and I'd look after myself. I'd get a job or something. I'd figure it out. But then I thought that Mum and Dad would find me too easily and I'd have to go back home. I then figured that since I was going to be at home forever, it would be better not to be around any more.' She stopped and started to cry.

'By "around any more", you mean take you own life with the pills you took?'

'Yeah, that's right. I know Mum takes sleeping tablets sometimes, so I got them and a whole bunch of Panadol and swallowed them with some Bourbon. I'm not sure what happened except I must have fallen asleep and then I woke up at the hospital. Now you're here.'

'So there was this moment you mentioned before where you said you thought you would be at home forever and

Chapter 7

that realisation made you decide to swallow the pills in the hope that you would die? Is that right? So you figured that with your mum and dad saying you couldn't move out, that would be a permanent thing? So in your mind that meant you would be there forever? Is that the case?'

'Ummm, I guess so. But when you say it like that, it doesn't sound right.'

'What I'm trying to do is to help you realise when exactly you decided to make the choice to end your life. You need to understand the reason yourself before you can really make sense of the whole thing. You also need to understand whether you still want to die or whether you wish to carry on living. That's a decision only you can make. Do you hear me? Only you can make that decision. No one else can.'

'I guess that was the point when I thought I'd do it. It was when I got the shits and panicked a bit. I don't want to live with Mum and Dad forever and for a while that was all I could see. Maybe I was too quick. Maybe I, maybe I didn't think it through properly. Oh, I've really made a mess here.'

She began to cry afresh, tears rolling down her cheeks in rivulets. I sat in silence allowing her to cry because she needed to, needed to consider what she had done and to think about what might have happened. She stopped after a short while, sniffling still, then blew her nose a few times.

Hitting the wall

'I'm really sorry,' she whispered.

'Don't apologise to me,' I told her. 'There's no need to apologise to me. I'm going to speak to you a couple more times before you are discharged. You'll be here today but probably go home tomorrow. I'm going to step outside and speak to your parents for a minute. Is it ok to speak to them about what we've talked about today or I can keep it completely confidential? You're an adult now, so it's up to you. What do you think?'

'Oh, you can tell them everything 'cos I won't know what to say to them. Yeah, you speak to them first and then allow them in. Can I speak to my sister first? I really want to say sorry to her before Mum and Dad come in. Is that ok?'

'Sure, that's fine. I'll catch you later on.'

'Thanks, thanks a lot,' she said looking at me and half smiling.

'Relax, don't worry. You'll be fine,' I said as I left her. I spent the next half hour speaking with her mum and dad and her little sister. I explained that she wanted her sister to go in first. They all agreed and the sister went in.

I heard the sister say as she entered the room. 'I'm sorry I called you a bitch' were the last words I heard before the door closed.

What was this attempted suicide? A cry for help? Maybe

Chapter 7

an impulsive childish act? Either way, you can see there was a time when the young woman had options that narrowed through lack of critical thinking. Her emotions ran too high which reduced her options and shrank her choices to one. The point when she felt that she would have to live with her parents forever was too much for her to contemplate, so she decided to try to take her own life to escape 'the forever at home' option. Immature though that decision appears to be, it still led her to a very dangerous and possibly fatal outcome. Had her sister not arrived home, the family may have be thinking about her death and speaking to a funeral home.

When I spoke with young people in a similar situation, I would trace back their thinking, analyse their options at the time and establish the point when they had decided to suicide. It was a process designed to help them realise the implications of their own thinking and to take them back to a place where a different decision was again available; to take them back to a spot where a decision could be reached that was positive and far less dangerous and permanent.

I'm happy to say that this young woman lived. I saw her two years ago during a shopping trip. A woman tapped me on the shoulder and asked me if my name was John. I nodded and she told me that I had helped her when she was a kid. She said she was really happy and had two young children and

Hitting the wall

that life was good. I was thrilled to see she had developed into a lovely happy woman. Occasionally you get results like this.

• • •

I was in my late thirties when the thought of suicide came to me. I was in a bad place and I was terribly unhappy in my job. I had three young children and a lovely wife. On the face of things, I was doing just fine. I had doubts, doubts that seemed to come from my very being. They infected my thoughts and made me doubt all I had learned and all I had become. The doubts, brought about by work issues, began to affect everything in my life. My work was affected, and doubts plagued me constantly. I had changed jobs and was working in a temporary capacity with another organisation. I had some differences of opinion with some people there and felt trapped. I chose not to tell anyone which further isolated myself by not doing so. My years of keeping much of my emotions to myself were proving to be my undoing. I slid quietly and surely into a place of darkness, a place where the only respite involved my departure from this world. I thought that the world would be better without me. I never once thought that my death would be any more than a blip in the grand scheme of things.

I convinced myself that perhaps my wife would be a bit

Chapter 7

upset but I was sure she would soon find someone far better, a better husband, a kinder person, a better father to the kids. I still loved my wife and she never put any pressure on me. She had always been totally supportive. She would have been horrified if I had told her and would have gone to any lengths to ensure my safety. I somehow failed to acknowledge this which left me to my own dark thoughts. There was no area of my life that I could see as being valuable. I began to think that my existence was no longer important; that, in fact, my existence should be terminated.

I can examine my state now with a far greater degree of clarity. I failed to do that at the time. At the beginning of one particular week, I felt there were a few choices. Firstly, stay in the current job, secondly, try to get back to my other job, thirdly, look for other employment and lastly, end it all. I dismissed the notion of suicide initially. I had seen the impact of suicide on families and didn't wish to put my own through that pain. I explored options as to whether I could leave and go back to my other job but that didn't seem a likely option.

I was left with the choice of trying to find other work and I looked, albeit very briefly, at other employment opportunities. I had no success. I found out how much my wife and kids would get from life insurance and

Hitting the wall

superannuation and was pleased to see the sum. They would be able to cope adequately with the amount, pay off the mortgage and have money leftover. Armed with this information, I reached the conclusion that death would be a very good option. Sure, it would be initially upsetting for my family but in the medium to long term, it would be better for them. Of this, I had no doubt. I didn't think for one minute that I was hurting them. I never ever wanted to cause them any harm. My love was ever there for them and I didn't see my decision as causing them any great anguish. So Thursday came and I had decided to go to The Gap to jump off the cliff. It would be immediate and fatal. My body would almost certainly be visually unrecognisable and my dentist would provide the details for identification. It was, I considered, a sound plan. I decided to go there just on lunchtime. I went to the car park and began to drive out towards the eastern suburbs. I had been there often and knew where to go. I was feeling light headed and anxious, my mind spinning at a thousand miles an hour.

All sorts of things crossed my mind, mainly those people I cared about; my kids, my wife, my work colleagues. I began to picture the funeral and what it would be like. I thought to myself that at least some people would be there and be upset. I was in the Bondi area, not far from my destination when I

Chapter 7

received the call.

'Hi, there's been a murder of a girl interstate but her parents live here. We'd like you to go and see the parents. They live in the eastern suburbs. I'll give you the address.'

Though I have other thoughts on my mind, I was quickly back in work mode and agreed to go and speak with them. They needed help and I was someone who could try to help alleviate their pain. I turned the car around and headed off to the address.

I rang the doorbell and an elderly man opened the door. 'Hello,' I said, 'my name is John Merrick. I'm the counsellor. The police mentioned that I would be coming, is that right?'

'Yes, of course, please come in, John.'

He was a man in his late sixties, a man whose face was etched with lines. He smiled as he showed me through to the small living area. His wife sat on a lounge chair, her eyes red from crying.

'Hello,' I said, 'my name is John and I'm the counsellor the police mentioned.' She rose from her chair and extended her hand to me.

'Thank you so much for coming,' she said in a weary tone.

'I'm very sorry for your loss,' I responded easily falling straight into help mode.

'Thank you. That's very kind of you,' she said.

Hitting the wall

'Please sit down,' said the man, motioning to a comfortable looking, well-used armchair. 'We do not often get visitors. It is nice of you to come. We only heard the news this morning. Our lovely Anna. She is, was, a beautiful girl.' He looked away and wiped away a tear. 'Sorry for my tears. She is our only child and this is such terrible news for us. We don't know what to do. We are not sure what to do next. I was hoping you could tell us and help us. If you would be so kind.'

'Yes, of course. I'll find out what I can and help you with any arrangements you need to make. I can certainly do that for you. That's no trouble,' I assured him.

I spent the next few hours with the family, occasionally making phone calls to police officers and forensic medicine people in the other state. Each time I would make these calls about their daughter, the parents would patiently sit and listen in to what I was saying, smiling encouragingly as if to thank me for my efforts.

'Ok, this is what is happening at the moment. There are some things I am about to tell you that are a little blunt but what I tell you is the truth as far as I am able to work out. Now, when I spoke with the forensic people, they told me they are going to perform an autopsy tomorrow morning. Do you know what an autopsy is? Do you need any information

Chapter 7

about that?' I asked gently.

'Please tell us what this is. I have some idea and my wife, she probably knows more than me, but I want to be sure what they are doing to her.'

'Yes, of course. When they do an autopsy, they do a large medical examination on her. They look at her body first, take any measurements and note any marks or cuts on her. The police have told me that there are some stab wounds, probably from a knife in her chest. I'm not sure how many.' They both put their hands up to their mouths at that.

'Oh, my God, our poor girl. How could anyone do that to her? How could they?' They both were showing signs of stress at the thought of their daughter being attacked.

'I know. It seems very hard to understand what and why this has happened. Shall I carry on?' They nodded.

'When the doctor has finished doing an external examination, they make large incisions in the body and examine her internally, looking for signs of trauma, or any illness that may be present. Basically they are making sure they examine her very thoroughly. They need to do this to gather all the evidence to establish a cause of her death so when they charge this person who has done this, they can make sure that the person does not get off the charge because we didn't get enough evidence. We don't want someone to get

Hitting the wall

off because evidence of her cause of death was not collected properly. Now, you need to know that the incisions they make are very long. They go from around the neck in a large Y shape down past her belly button. They also cut around the back of the head and skull and examine her brain to make sure no trauma was done to the head. In a sense, it is like a very big operation by a specialist doctor. Does that make sense to you both?'

They both stared at me listening intently but both were clearly very emotional. I was telling them their daughter was going to be subject to a very large-scale operation and they were wanting to know as much as they could.

'I understand, John. You need to do this thing to make sure that the man who did this deed will not escape. Have I got this right?'

I nodded my agreement. 'Yes, that's right. Would you like to know what happens next? I can provide some information for you about this if you like.'

'Yes, please. When we can we get our daughter back please, John?'

I went on and explained the process to them. I told them of the need to establish a clear cause of death and the necessity of conducting an autopsy. The identification would need to be done but this was being done through a review of dental

Chapter 7

records that the police had already obtained.

I explained that sometimes the dead person would have to be kept at the morgue for a time because initial investigations may require further examination of the body for the sake of matching up injuries with any statements or admissions. Finally, the body would be released and they could arrange a funeral.

They sat quietly and attentively as I went through as much as I could. They asked questions and I did what I could do to help them understand. I spoke briefly about my wife and my three children as I felt that knowing me a little more might help them understand me as a man and as someone wanting to help. As I left the unit, I thanked them for their hospitality, coffee and delicious homemade biscuits that they had provided during my visit.

'No, no, John. It is we who need to thank you. You have come to us. You have helped us and you have explained to us what we can do now. You have helped us in our hour of need. You are a gentleman, John, someone who is kind and wise. I will never forget you and what you have done for us. I hope you and your wife and three boys have long and happy lives. You really deserve every blessing God can grant you. I will call you tomorrow as you said. Thank you again.'

As I left, his words rang in my ears like a bell. I did not

Hitting the wall

deserve such words of praise, did I? I had done my job as best I could but this father's words still echoed in my head, and then slowly down into my heart. It was such a kind thing to say in his hour of distress. He had made me feel special for being there to help him. I felt I had done something good and right. I had helped them. I had provided support and information and that had actually helped them. I seemed to be thinking at the speed of light. And then it came to me.

'What the hell were you thinking?' I said out loud to myself. 'What the hell were you going to do. You idiot,' I admonished myself. I had no desire to die any more. I want to live. I want to see my wife and my kids. I want to see my kids grow up. I want to spend the rest of my hopefully long life with Helen. What on earth was I thinking?

I went home and spoke with Helen about what I had thought of doing. She took me to task about it. She told me if I ever was upset, that I must promise to talk with her. Straightforward advice that I would heed. When I think back at that time, I can only think that Anna's death in some way, saved my life. I'm not sure I would have jumped off The Gap. I'm not sure whether I would have left Helen and the kids. All I know now is that I am very fortunate to be living and breathing. I am ever grateful to this day to be alive with my wife and children.

Chapter 7

Anna's body was returned to Sydney a week later. The family invited me to the funeral but I declined their kind invitation. I never did find out the full details of why Anna was killed partly because she had been murdered interstate and the trial was held interstate too. However, I did find out later that the killer was given twenty years imprisonment for her murder.

Suicide has not crossed my mind since. Lessons I learnt from that episode helped me to develop skills that have worked to keep me well mentally and physically. I have learnt to talk about times when I become morose or unhappy. I actually tell people when I am feeling low. That's a big change for me. I can understand only too well how people get so far down that they are unable to see any future. I believe it has also helped me to help others who have suicidal thoughts. I feel I know some of what they are experiencing. If you get that low, or even before you get there, ring someone, ring anyone. I can tell you, you leave nothing but misery and despair for those left behind. I know. I've seen it and felt it.

Hitting the wall

Many counselling services operate 24/7. Here are three.

Beyond Blue: 1300 22 4636 (specialising in suicide prevention)

Lifeline: 13 11 14

1800RESPECT: 1800 737 732

CHAPTER 8

A CHILD'S BRUTAL MURDER: A MOTHER'S RESPONSE

I did a job once that showed me how it takes a village to heal a soul.

I'm sitting around a table outside in the cold of winter. I can see my breath as it steams from my mouth. I laugh at a joke that someone tells. I sip at a glass of red wine, cold to the touch as I lift it to my lips.

'I still think smoking a pipe makes you look at least twenty per cent wiser at least,' I say as I draw the smoke into my mouth. 'You see, just doing that, it really makes you look wiser.'

'Absolutely,' agrees John, my fellow pipe smoking buddy

Chapter 8

as he draws on his pipe, grinning wickedly. There are four of us sitting at an outside table at the Outsider Gallery, a coffee shop at Captains Flat, a small town about a half hour's drive from Canberra. It's a small place; much smaller than during the gold rush in the 1880s and '90s. Now a one pub town with the longest bar in the Southern Hemisphere, it has a small community centre, an old Post Office that no longer serves its original purpose, homes scattered across the valley and one quirky looking set of buildings belonging to Christine Simpson, the mother of Ebony Simpson and Gunther Deix, her partner. Their place is purple coloured, decorated with paintings and the garden full of sculptures. An amazing place, once a coffee shop and restaurant, it is now a gallery, full of paintings and other works done by Gunther and sculptures done by Christine. Nudes adorn the walls inside the gallery, paintings of bush settings, and at the back, a picture of Christine painted by Gunther. The place is nestled at the base of a large hill and trees overlook the property as they climb towards the summit. It's a peaceful place, quite at odds with its owners' tale.

I only saw Ebony once. She had been admitted to the morgue and my colleague had come upstairs to tell me that the body of a little girl had been found in a small dam. I went downstairs to the mortuary area and looked at the body. She

A child's brutal murder: a mother's response

was nine years old according to the police. She had been kidnapped and murdered. I only saw a glimpse of her; I noticed she has some leaves and some dirt on her and she was very wet. The police and the undertaker contractors had brought her in and were completing the requisite paperwork. No one said much.

The police were still conducting their investigations and were fairly tight lipped about their opinions. I went back upstairs and thought about the parents of the young girl. I thought that I would contact them soon and get their details from the investigating detectives. I rang the detectives the next day to get the telephone number for the parents. The police mentioned that the parents were coping, that they didn't want to be disturbed and that they were receiving support from extended family and friends. I accepted what they said. To be honest, I wasn't insistent. I learned a lesson that day. I should have been more insistent; I should have contacted the parents even given the advice by the police not to. I merely accepted their statement and heard nothing until two weeks later. This story, though, is not about Ebony. It is about the living, those left behind by murder, in particular, Christine, Ebony's mother.

The first contact came when I received a phone call from Peter, Ebony's father. He was angry and asked me why no

Chapter 8

one had contacted the Simpson family. He went on to say that everyone else who had been involved in the search for her at the time had received support and counselling. He demanded why no one had been in touch with them. I tried to explain why I had not called but my reason sounded trite even as I spoke the words. He didn't accept the reasons and demanded that the family get counselling and assistance. I organised a time when I could go and see them at their farmhouse in Bargo, south west of Sydney, a drive of a little over an hour from the Glebe morgue. As I headed down the highway, I didn't realise what a change this meeting would bring to my life. When I met Peter, he was still angry and really gave me a telling off. I said I would do what I could to help.

My usual routine for seeing families was to offer counselling, maybe once a fortnight. They could either travel to Sydney for the sessions or I could come out every second visit. I now realise how pathetic that sounds. Their whole world had been upended and here I was saying to them; why not just come to Sydney, travel down the highway and come and see me for an hour. It makes me realise how little I understood then compared to what I now know. Christine didn't say much that first day. I do remember her face and her sorrow. Her eyes spoke of devastation. Her face drawn,

A child's brutal murder: a mother's response

an almost haunted look, as if she had seen the end of the world and didn't have the words to express the horror she had witnessed.

Something touched me that day but I didn't know what it was. I didn't often feel completely useless but this was one such time. I drove back to Sydney and told my colleague, Deborah, about what I had seen. She was supportive and listened. We both agreed that maybe more could be done but we didn't quite know what.

I saw the Simpson family soon after that. Christine and Peter made the effort to travel to Sydney to see me, not that they were happy about having to do so. They made that quite clear during the hour-long session. I realised the process I usually followed wasn't working for these parents. There had to be more I could do. I spent the next couple of weeks trying to work out what that might be but all I drew was a blank.

Two weeks later, I travelled to Bargo to see them again. I wasn't looking forward to it given that things had not gone very well up to this point. I knew that my offerings were not enough. On this occasion, I spent time with Christine. She spoke as if her heart had been ripped from her chest, her eyes so full of pain. We spoke about the support that she and her family needed. I realised that they needed far more than

Chapter 8

I could ever provide. They needed to be able to share their pain with someone who could really understand what it is like when your child has been murdered. As I drove back down the highway to Glebe, a thought began to germinate. What if they spoke to someone who had undergone a similar tragedy; what if they could speak to someone who understood their pain far better than I. For some reason, I began to think about possibilities as to who might be able to help them who had undergone a similar experience, people who had experienced the death of someone through murder.

Garry Lynch and his wife sprang to mind. Garry and Grace Lynch's daughter, Anita Cobby had been brutally murdered some years before. Garry had gone on to do work with offenders and had been very involved in the serious offenders review board. I thought that I would contact Mr Lynch and ask him if he would be willing to speak with the Simpson family. I found his number in the phone book and called. He answered jovially. He told me that he had never spoken to a counsellor before. I was amazed at this. Anita Cobby's case was so well known in Australia, it was staggering to hear that no counsellor had ever spoken to him or his wife. He went on to tell me that the police had spoken to him but no counsellor had ever rung the family to enquire as to their wellbeing.

A child's brutal murder: a mother's response

I asked him whether he would be willing to travel to Bargo and speak with Peter and Christine. He was a friendly open man and he immediately accepted my suggestion. I told him I would speak with the parents and get their permission to pass on the their details to Mr Lynch. As I hung up, I thought that this idea really might be just the thing to help the Simpsons. I rang Peter soon after and spoke of my idea. He seemed accepting of the notion so I called Garry soon after. Garry and Grace arranged to go to Bargo the following day. I heard from Peter and Christine soon after. They said that it had been very helpful; that it was very comforting to know that what they were feeling was not unusual and was quite normal. My idea began to take shape. I decided that people with lived shared experience might benefit from speaking and listening to each other. The idea would gradually turn into the Homicide Victims Support Group, a group that exists until this day.

I received a call from the police about four months after Ebony was murdered. They told me that Christine wanted to know the details as to what had happened to Ebony. This was something I had not spoken about with Christine or Peter and when it was mentioned, we simply did not talk about the specific details. It was as if silence was preferable; the truth might be too horrific. The police seemed to think

Chapter 8

the same way. They didn't feel it was necessary to provide complete details as they were anxious not to distress Christine any further. I felt that she had the right to know as much as she wanted so I volunteered to meet with her and go through the autopsy report.

All autopsy reports contain the brutal details, injury patterns, swabs taken, the weight of individual organs and much more. A forensic pathologist had done the investigation but then other samples are retained and sent for further examination such as microbiology, toxicology and the like. Toxicology tests can determine toxins in the system and microbiological testing can determine the presence of diseases such as Hepatitis C and HIV. The reports also determine the presence of other bodily fluids, such as semen. I went through the autopsy report and received a run down from the forensic pathologist in charge. I also spoke with the forensic biologist who had performed the testing. By the time I finished, I had a very good idea what had happened. I drove to Bargo to meet with Christine.

The day was warm and sunny and we sat outside, the warmth providing some comfort against the cold hard facts that I was about to relay. It was hard to know where to begin but somehow I did. I asked her whether she really wanted to know what had happened, whether she wanted to know all the details. She told

A child's brutal murder: a mother's response

me she needed to understand exactly what happened because she was imagining a thousand things that had happened to her daughter and the truth would allow her to put to rest the stories and images that went around and around in her head. She needed to know the truth and said, 'Besides, it's my right as Ebony's mum'.

'What I'm about to tell you is really heard to hear. It gives details about what happened to Ebony and may be really awful for you to hear. If at any time, you want me to stop for a break or you want me to stop altogether, just say so. If it becomes too much, just tell me to stop. Is that ok with you?' She nodded.

To say that the story of Ebony's murder is bleak is a gross understatement. Ebony had been bound with wire and raped. Her schoolbag was weighted down and she was thrown into the dam. The cause of death was drowning. She had been alive when she went into the dam. I went through the report, often stopping as Christine cried at what she had heard. It took hours to go through but at the end, she now knew exactly what had happened to her daughter. I felt unclean. How could any man do that to a child? I could not comprehend the actions of someone like this. I apologised for being the one to tell her the painful reality about what happened but she said she had needed this information,

Chapter 8

to help her understand and to help her deal with it. Her imagination would no longer be filled with images of what might have happened. She now knew the stark reality. I have never forgotten that day. The warmth of the day, the bench upon which we sat and the horrible graphic story of this man's actions against a defenceless nine-year-old girl.

I spent much of the next months working on a structure and plan for the new group. Many people, ex-coroners, the current state coroner, police officers and family members of victims worked tirelessly to make the group a reality. Naturally, Peter and Christine and Garry and Grace Lynch were members of the organising committee. Support, education and change were the words to describe its ideals. Support for those left behind, education for those involved in the criminal justice system and change to the system; changes that could include both legislative and procedural.

During this time, many of the organising committee decided that there was much to change for family members of homicide victims. Some legislation had to be changed, they argued. I tended to agree but I decided we would have no real platform until we had spoken to other members who may well join. I enlisted the help of a remarkable woman who had been involved in another bereavement support group. Martha tirelessly contacted families voluntarily and

A child's brutal murder: a mother's response

did so with great skill and compassion. She could work the room like no other I had met. With the support of many, she and others made the Homicide Victims Support Group a reality with the first meeting being held in 1993, less than a year after Ebony was murdered.

I saw Christine regularly. She attended committee meetings and the like. I still spoke with her in a counselling role and it was clear she was still finding life incredibly hard. The trial of Garforth, the offender, was certainly uppermost on her mind. There is no doubt she was seething with anger about what he had done – completely understandable. I could see how much she hurt and I could well understand her fury at him. 'I'd be angry too, Chris,' I told her at more than one meeting.

Christine's response is not unusual although, as a society, we expect people to get over serious trauma 'and get on with it'. We don't really like people to be angry for long often making comments about how bad it is to hang on to anger, how it only hurts the person and so on. Sometimes I got the impression that others wanted her to be more forgiving. I remember distinctly some of people expressing the sentiment that she can never heal until she learned to forgive. I may well have taken that position before I met Christine, but that relationship has made me change my mind and reassess my views.

Chapter 8

Garforth was found guilty and sentenced to life imprisonment. Peter and Christine were supported through the court process by family and friends and at the end of the trial, Peter made a statement outside court. He said that the Simpson family was serving the life sentence and that Garforth was getting bed and breakfast. There was still that intense anger present. Legal appeals were made on behalf of Garforth but fortunately they were dismissed. To date, Garforth is going to remain in jail for the rest of his life.

Christine and Peter attended the Homicide Victims Support Group meetings regularly and often provided support to other families who joined the group. I left the group and lost touch with Christine. This wasn't through any choice made by either of us. Like a lot of things in life, it just happened. I heard that Christine and Peter had separated. I wasn't surprised as this is a common occurrence among those who have lost children, particularly in horrific circumstances. I sometimes wondered what had happened to her. I had always imagined in my head that we would keep in touch but we hadn't. Then, out of the blue, I received a call from Christine one afternoon.

She said she was nearby our home but didn't know the exact address. I immediately invited her for dinner hoping that she would be able to make it. She arrived and I was very

A child's brutal murder: a mother's response

happy to see her. She told me that she had been living pretty rough and, at times, even lived in her car. I invited her to stay the night. I wanted her to have a safe place for at least one night. She deserved that after all her suffering and loss. She stayed and we bid each other goodbye in the morning. She told me she wasn't sure what she was going to do but she would see what life had in store. She said she was going to her sister Marg's place and would do something there. Again, I lost touch with her.

I then heard she was in a relationship with a man, Gunther Deix, an artist from the Southern Highlands in New South Wales. He had asked to paint a portrait of her. She had agreed to this request on one condition. If she didn't like it, he had to burn it. She liked it and they began a relationship. I only heard later that some of her family and friends were not too thrilled about the relationship. I was told they didn't really approve of his bohemian nature.

Nevertheless, it worked for Christine and Gunther. They found a property in Captains Flat and immediately went to work, creating a gallery and restaurant. Christine is a cook with a great deal of skill, and it wasn't long before people started coming there through word of mouth. Gunther's artwork was much admired and together they began to grow a successful business. I saw the portrait that

Chapter 8

Gunther had painted of Christine. I immediately looked at how he had recreated Christine's eyes. Yes, there was the unmistakeable pain I had seen through the years I had known her. I looked at the eyes and knew he had captured her heart and her soul. I have seen pain over the years, incalculable pain, pain that would tear at the very fabric of someone's being, pain that would kill and destroy if it was left to its own devices.

At the same time, I could see in that face in the painting a love for Ebony – a love for other things – I'm not certain. The heart shape of the face seemed to symbolise hope; a hope that life could one day be bearable, maybe even good. Then I noticed another face in the painting. In the bottom left of the portrait, there was a face, coloured red, filled with anger and devastation, mouth agape screaming. I recognised the anger. Christine had always expressed her anger and had always told me she had every right to do so. Talon-like fingers tore at the flesh of the face in agony. The portrait had captured the despair, sadness and anger that Christine carried within her. It captured the legacy of a murdered daughter and the ripples of pain that had been caused by that one horrendous act. But it also captured the love and hope that is very much a part of Christine too.

Again, some years passed and I heard that the gallery and

A child's brutal murder: a mother's response

restaurant were faring well. I received a call from Christine out of the blue one day. We spoke about what she had been doing and how she was spending her life now with Gunther. She went on to say that they were planning an art exhibition for murder victims and they were hoping I would attend and say a few words. Why me? I thought at the time. I was thrilled to be asked and I immediately agreed. She explained the exhibition was a series of boxes attached to the gallery walls, each containing words and images of the victim. Some had stories of the feelings of the family left behind. It sounded as though it would be a moving display. Christine told me that she had invited families of the victims and many of them would be in attendance. The exhibition would be held in late August around the time of the anniversary of Ebony's death. Both Helen and I had been invited and so it was a Saturday afternoon as we wound our way down the highway from Sydney to Captains Flat.

It was bitterly cold as we drove into the main street of the township. I saw the gallery for the first time and was struck by the vibrant colours and the nudes adorning the glass panels that opened into the courtyard alongside. It seemed oddly out of place in this small town. We went inside and went straight to Christine. I embraced her and she smiled. She looked different somehow. Some of the pain in her eyes

Chapter 8

that was previously omnipresent had gone. Yes, there was still pain in the eyes, but less so. I shook Gunther's hand and was struck by his warmth and welcoming personality. There were many people there, milling around inside the restaurant area, each sharing stories and meeting new people. The exhibition itself was in an annexe, across the courtyard. Inside a warm log fire crackled away opposite the entrance. Along the wall and from the ceiling were small boxes, each with photographs and words, descriptions of lives being snatched from this earth.

I looked around the room seeing that much of the space was taken with these boxes. I didn't count them and as I walked around the space, I inspected each of them carefully. I recognised many of the people and their families. Some of the images took me back to the times when I first met the families, either through counselling or through the homicide victims group. I was overwhelmed. People approached me warmly and I introduced myself to some of them. That night I met some of Christine's friends and her family. I warmed to many of them and they were extraordinarily welcoming. Many thanked me for the things I had done for Christine. I felt uncomfortable at the praise I received and generally turned the conversation to something else. I became nervous at the prospect of speaking to the group feeling vulnerable

A child's brutal murder: a mother's response

at the prospect of addressing those who had both witnessed suffering and had felt it first hand.

I had planned a speech but the words now seemed vacuous and meaningless. I had a few glasses of wine to ward off the cold and to get a small dose of Dutch courage. At Christine's orders, we all gathered in the annexe and stood in a circle, mirroring the display itself. I said some words from my heart praising the work Gunther had done and thanking both of them for the kind invitation. Relieved to have finished, I headed outside to the courtyard and spoke at greater length with some of Christine's friends and family. We sat in small groups around the logs that burned brightly inside the clay chimenias. Invariably the conversations focused on Christine, her life and losses. People really felt for her, but they didn't talk of her pain or her sorrow, but of her strength, her willingness to help others, her love for her children and Gunther. The focus was not on loss but on her life, her desire and passion for change and her desire to live life to the full.

As I glanced around the gallery and the courtyard, I saw a large number of nudes, in bush settings, some near creeks, some reclining on chairs. Each image had a startling resemblance to Christine. Christine came out to join one of the groups and I asked her if the paintings were of her. She laughed and told me she modelled nude for Gunther and

Chapter 8

she had often gone into the bush while he painted her. She still found it rewarding and exhilarating.

The night passed with too many drinks and too much good food. Despite the fact that the night was an exhibition of murder and the anniversary of Ebony's death, the night was filled with laughter, interspersed with some tears. On the return journey, Helen and I spoke of the people we had met. We swapped stories trying at times to work out who fitted in where and who was who.

I received another call in May the following year and to my delight, we were invited again. I was asked to say a few words and I again agreed immediately. The night was spent renewing acquaintances and meeting new people. I watched the interactions taking place around me, people laughing, telling jokes, but somehow bound together with a common purpose. Many of them had a story that involved a life being violently taken, but each willing to listen to each other's pain, a shared painful experience. Again, however, the mood was uplifting but when the situation warranted, there were hugs and some tears. It was a place where you could share your story. People understood each other's pain without the need to go through it in forensic detail.

I began to develop an understanding of the nature of evenings such as these. It wasn't about the people who had

A child's brutal murder: a mother's response

died; it was about the living. Like funerals, the event existed to allow the living to reflect in some fashion to exchange stories about the person who had died and to explain a little about their sorrow and pain. More than that however, it encouraged the expression of emotions, normalising feelings and providing genuine sympathy towards each other.

Late in the evening, I approached Christine and asked her how she was doing. We spoke openly and honestly how she felt and what was happening for her. She would often say to me how she woke up crying in the middle of the night, how she couldn't understand how and why she was still alive. She told me of her love for her sons and how she worried about their futures. She said that she felt many people didn't understand the numbers of people affected by a single murder, how the ripples from a death can cause so much damage. Not only were her sons affected, but also their partners, their kids were all touched by one senseless act of violence. She said how hard it still was for her at times to get out of bed, to work and to live life. She told me how much she hated Garforth and wished that she could kill him. The anger was always there. We spoke at length about the hatred she felt.

I didn't once argue with her about the nature of her anger and hatred towards him. I understood the depth of her

Chapter 8

passion and told her I would feel the same way if anything happened to my kids. I occasionally said a few things but more often than not, I listened to her and sat with her. We would sit, a glass of wine never far away, and sometimes she would cry, her face fallen as she remembered Ebony and what she had meant to her. She cried as she spoke about the first years after Ebony had been murdered, how she couldn't get out of bed; even brushing her teeth became something that was all too hard. She glanced around and then spoke of her current life. Her new life with Gunther, Captains Flat, her friends and family, what it all meant to her.

She didn't speak despairingly, nor in a voice with any great sense of hope, but one of certainty; a tacit acceptance of her life. Certain aspects of her life were positive, others appalling. Still, she understood her life, more so than many others. Her pain and her loss had not stopped her from living life. She did so in many ways more fully and more vibrantly than many who had never faced such obstacles. Maybe because she had faced her daughter's murder, she could love and live more fiercely. Perhaps the loss had in some fashion triggered risk taking within her that allowed her to live her full life. Since fear no longer was a factor, she could take risks and do things that many shun. Small things like bills and financial stressors were no longer a serious concern. 'Who cares?' she

A child's brutal murder: a mother's response

would say. 'What are they gonna' do? Chase me down? Let them try. Nothing can hurt me more than I've already been.' She was probably right. Maybe nothing more could hurt her.

I kept going to Captains Flat every year. The numbers began to diminish and the group comprised more and more of family and friends. I witnessed the nature of relationships and saw how each of them made a difference in her life; how each friend and family member had their own unique role to play.

So here I am sitting outside around the fire, telling stories, laughing at some old joke listening to people share tales. It is 2016 and we have been coming since 2007. I have developed relationships with some of the friends and family. They too have developed their own friendships as a result of the annual memorial. Christine comes out into the cold. 'Look. Here are all the troublemakers. You still out here drinking wine?'

'No, we were sipping water and indulging in polite conversation,' says one wit. I smile at her arrival. Watching the interaction makes me think of an old African proverb. Its origin is unclear but it was used widely in the late 20th and early 21st centuries. 'It takes a village to raise a child' is a term used to infer that no person is an island. A community is required to help nurture a child to grow. The term could be used in the case of a tragic murder; 'it takes a village to

Chapter 8

heal a soul'. Artistic license aside, the thought seems to ring true to me. I watched as the relationships helped the healing process for Christine.

Each relationship had and still has its own flavour, its own dynamics. It may be the late night phone calls when one is feeling down, it might be the dinner where distraction is the order of the day, it might be some words of wisdom that ring true and help in a particular dilemma. Either way, each unique relationship helps in the long-term process of healing. I have seen first hand the nature of some of these relationships and witnessed the healing that comes from these interactions. I have watched children growing up around the group and they too have helped in the healing process. New life has breathed life into some older life. I have watched Christine with her grandchildren and seen their healing power.

One of the most significant elements in healing for Christine appears to be the unconditional love Gunther has for her. On the face of things, Gunther appears eccentric; an alternate artist, unconventional in many ways. Whilst this is true, the banter and gentle teasing that occurs highlights their love for one another. Barely an hour goes by without one of them ribbing each other. Always done with good humour and gentle intent, the two of them seem at ease with

A child's brutal murder: a mother's response

each other. No hurtful or disparaging comments are made. There is genuine love in the expressions on their faces when they look at each other.

I have now known Christine for about 24 years. I first met her some weeks after Ebony was murdered. I still remember distinctly the pain in her eyes; the haunted look that still sticks in my mind. I had doubts back then that she would ever or could ever live life again. Her appearance was so fragile. I thought that she would snap like a twig. I sensed that she might not live long. I felt that I could offer so little to her. All my counselling skills and experience really came to nothing. I'm tempted to say that I threw the book out of the window but that would make me appear far more daring and brave than I actually was. I am no saint, but when I witnessed this woman suffering from such indescribable pain, I knew that something had to change. It was when I became passionate, when I let my guard down, that I really began to make a difference.

Christine is a warrior; fearless, honest and willing to tilt at any windmill. She faces any challenges with equanimity whether it be facing the media or meeting the premiers of state governments. She does so with calmness, a sense of strength and a sense of justice. In my younger days, I had the sense that anger was dangerous. Anger would never lead to

Chapter 8

a sense of peace. Anger was something that would gradually eat away at you, causing an inability to heal and move forward. I never considered that someone could do both. Christine has taught me numerous lessons. One that rings very true is that Christine has steadfastly remained angry towards both the injustice of a young life being taken so horrifically and towards Garforth, the man who committed the crime. She has maintained that fury until this day. This hasn't prevented her from living life and loving those around her. It has not stopped her creating, working and developing life in her own fashion. The passion in which she lives her life is just as obvious as her anger as is her love for her family and friends. Christine told me she went to see the premier of New South Wales one day. She was making a particular point and she had brought a photograph of Ebony that she placed on the desk, Ebony's smiling face looking straight at the premier. As Christine was leaving, the premier asked her not to forget the photo. Christine told him to keep it as a reminder.

In my life, I have had the good fortune of meeting and growing close to two extraordinarily strong women – I married one and I am firm friends with the other.

A child's brutal murder: a mother's response

Homicide Victims Support Group
Level 2, 239 Church Street, Parramatta, NSW 2150
Tel: 02 8833 8400 or 1800 191 777
Website: hvsg.com.au

Victims of Crime Assistance League
1/432 Hunter Street, Newcastle NSW 2300
Tel: (02) 4926 2711
Website: vocal.org.au

Enough is Enough
Shop 2
10–14 Boyle Street, Sutherland 2232
Tel: (02) 9542 4029
Website: enoughisenough.org.au

CHAPTER 9

A TRAGIC CRASH; A YOUNG WIDOW'S NIGHTMARE

I did a job once where I learned a lot about young love, death and the dating scene.

When I first started working at the morgue, I had been married for five years. I hadn't dated anyone except my wife since 1979. I had met her at university and we had been together ever since, despite her attempts at dumping me on occasion. In other words, I had not dated another woman for a long time. But what would happen if something happened to my marriage? I couldn't imagine it. I found out what it was like for one young woman.

'We've got an MVA downstairs', my colleague said as

Chapter 9

she wandered in. MVA is shorthand that we use for motor vehicle accident. 'Young man, killed. Has a young wife. She's coming in to do the ID. Can you do it for me? I've got a counselling session in about half and hour and I don't want to get caught up with the ID downstairs.'

'Sure, that's fine. I'll go down now and get him set up. Do we know anything more apart from the fact he's young and has a wife?'

'No idea. Just got told a few minutes ago and the police wanted someone to be with her. They said she's pretty fragile and they're worried about how she'll cope.'

'Going down now,' I saluted and took off downstairs. The young man's body was already in the viewing room. He had some nasty lacerations on his face but aside from that, he looked as though he could be visually identified. I grabbed some rubber gloves, as I always did. We often touched bodies and today was no different. I reached under the blanket and took out his hand so the wife could hold it if she chose to. I had a good look at him. I wanted to describe him to her before she saw him.

The preparation before the viewing is always vital. I went through a quick checklist. Ok, his head appears undamaged; he has a laceration below his right eye, he has a cut on his nose that looks a bit nasty, he has a cut on his chin and his

A tragic crash; a young widow's nightmare

hair is messed up. He looks like he has a full head of hair and he looked to be in his late twenties, maybe early thirties. His eyes were open, often disconcerting for families. I took his top eyelid and placed it under the bottom eyelid. Often this worked, occasionally it didn't. This time however, his eyes remained shut. Good, I thought. He looks ok now.

I went to the office where I grabbed the paperwork. He was twenty-seven years old, had a wife Sharon and had crashed on a major road in south-western Sydney. According to the police report, he had veered on to the wrong side of the road and had collided with a large truck. He was pronounced dead at the scene of the accident. Poor bastard, I thought. So young. His wife can't be much older. Sometimes it doesn't seem fair. How is she going to cope with her husband's death at such a young age? I guess I'll find out soon enough.

A woman in her mid to late twenties came through the door, followed by two police officers and an older man, probably in his late fifties, early sixties. The police officer closest to her said something to her and she sat on one of the chairs in the waiting room, head bowed and visibly upset. She placed her head in the palms of her hands and bent forward so her elbows rested on her knees. The older man approached her and placed his hand on her shoulder, a little awkwardly, as if the touch wasn't easy for him. The young

Chapter 9

woman didn't look up. She sat, head down. This will be her. I approached the door into the waiting area and greeted the police officers and invited them in.

'Hi, I'm John, the counsellor. Are you the guys from the MVA?'

'Yeah. Hi, I'm Craig and this is Jason. Thanks for being here, mate. Appreciate it. The bloke's wife, Sharon, is the lady over there.' He turned his head towards the waiting room. 'She's really a mess. The bloke with her is her dad, Barry. Good bloke, really keen to help his daughter out. We brought him along too to help her with the ID. We thought he might do the ID instead of Sharon, you know, to save her the pain and distress.'

'Thanks guys, appreciate it. I'll just go and speak with them now and take them through into the anteroom before we do the ID in the viewing area. He's all set up in there, so we're right to go. You guys stay here until we do the ID. Is that ok?'

'Suits us. You do what you need to do and sing out when we need to get the ID statement signed.' I nodded and walked into the waiting room.

'Hi, I'm John, a counsellor here. Would you like to come into the other waiting area? It's a bit more private.'

Sharon looked up at me. She had obviously been crying,

A tragic crash; a young widow's nightmare

her eyes red and cheeks damp. I shook Barry's hand. 'Please come through over here.' I motioned to a small door.

'Wait a minute, please.' It was Barry and he sounded frightened.

'Sharon doesn't have to come in and see him. I said to the police I would do the identification so …' He stopped.

'I understand Barry. This room isn't where he is. It's a smaller waiting room where we can sit and talk before you see him. Come on, let's all go in.' I walked slowly to the door and opened it, allowing them to walk ahead of me as I held open the door.

'Please sit down.' I motioned to the chairs. Sharon resumed her position in another chair, again with her head in her hands and bent over with her elbows resting on her knees. I looked at them in turn as Barry looked more and more terrified.

'There's a few things I'd like to explain before we go into the room. The door just behind me is the viewing room. We'll go in there soon but first I want to explain what he looks like and what the room looks like so you're not surprised or shocked. Ok?'

Sharon looked up. 'I don't know if I can see him. I don't know if I'd handle it. I'm so scared,' she said as she began to cry.

Chapter 9

'I know it can be scary. It's really awful what has happened. I'm so sorry for your loss. My most sincere condolences to you both.'

They looked at me and smiled slightly. 'Thanks John,' said Barry. Sharon looked down again and resumed her position. Barry spoke. 'John, I told the police I would do the identification like I said before. I don't want Shaz to do it. She's too upset already.'

I had heard this so many times before, well-intentioned family members trying to save someone's feelings by performing the legal requirement of the formal identification. Usually, a male member of the family would take it upon himself to volunteer. They would offer to spare the person, often a female relative from distress. I found over the years that this was not as helpful as it appeared.

I decided I wanted Sharon to know the facts and so be able to make an informed decision. In other words, I would describe the situation as best I could and let Sharon decide whether she wanted to proceed or not.

As with others in the same situation, knowing the facts can help the person to make the decision and not allow someone else to decide for them. So many times I had spoken to family members who had regretted not seeing their loved one after death. It happens that people who

A tragic crash; a young widow's nightmare

have been spared the ordeal of performing the identification can regret not doing so at a later date. Nearly all had told me that they wished they had seen the person who had died. They often said that they found it difficult to accept the death because they hadn't seen the body. I am not suggesting for one moment that this is right for everyone but I believe that people need to be given the opportunity to make an informed choice. An informed choice means that they are told what they will see, the room, the state of the body; the whole picture in detail. Then, and only then, can they make an informed decision. I felt really strongly about this and often had to argue with people to support the person in their right to see the dead person.

'Barry. Thanks so much for agreeing to do this for your daughter. You are really being very supportive of her. It's clear that you love Sharon and you don't want her to suffer. I understand that. I just need you to know some things before Sharon and you make that choice. Ok?' I immediately went on.

'Behind me through the door there is a smallish room. It's fairly dimly lit and it's a kind of pinkish colour. There is a wooden partition halfway in the room about four feet high. Behind the partition, you will see him lying on a hospital trolley. He is covered with a blue hospital blanket up to

Chapter 9

his neck. Ok so far? I've taken out one of his arms from under the blanket so you can hold his hand if you like. Now his face has got some cuts and lacerations.' I went through my checklist.

'He has a laceration below his right eye, he has a cut on his nose that looks a bit nasty, he has a cut on his chin. His hair is a ...'

'... a bit messy, isn't it,' said Sharon completing my sentence as she looked up at me. 'It was always such a mess, his hair. He always had really lovely long hair and I loved that it was wavy. I love his hair. I mean, I loved his hair.' She put an emphasis on loved. I understood what she meant.

'Yes, he's got a really full head of hair, that's for sure,' I agreed smiling gently. 'Also his eyes are closed,' I finished.

'I always thought that people were in small fridges like in the movies,' said Barry to no one in particular.

'Yes, a lot of people think they will go into a room full of fridges and we pull open a drawer to show the body. I think we're a lot more dignified than that. You need to be able to see him in a way that isn't horrible, even though what has happened is really horrible. One other really important thing is that he is cold. He's very cold to the touch. We keep people here under refrigerated conditions. If you want to touch him or kiss him, that's fine, but keep it in mind, he will

A tragic crash; a young widow's nightmare

be cold. Do either of you have any questions for me before we go in? Ask anything you like please.'

'Does he look peaceful?' Sharon asked. It was always such a hard question to answer. Did the body look peaceful? I'm not sure. Do dead bodies look peaceful as though they are asleep? What if I said yes and they said no he didn't. 'I'm not sure how to answer that. His eyes are closed and his face has some cuts and lacerations but aside from that, he looks as though he is resting. His face looks relaxed. I probably haven't answered the question very well. I'm sorry. I didn't know him in life, so I'm not sure whether to tell you he looks peaceful or not. Not knowing him, I don't know.'

It was about the most honest answer I could give. When people go in to view the person who has died, they often say that the person looks peaceful but I wasn't going to be the person who offered that opinion first. 'Look love,' said Barry 'you don't need to see him. It's best to remember him as he was, not as he's like now.'

It wasn't advice that I would give. Even though it came from a good place – Barry wanting to protect his daughter – the truth is I didn't believe it at all. I jumped in.

'That may not always be true, Barry. I've often found that people get enormous benefit from seeing the person who has died. People sometimes get a sense of peace when they are

Chapter 9

given the opportunity. It's completely your decision, Sharon. If you want to think about it for a while, that's fine. If you decide not to, that's fine too. You decide what's right for you.' Barry didn't look terribly happy with me but I didn't want her to regret her decision later.

'I don't know, Dad. I'll have a think.' She turned and faced me.

'Can Dad go in first and then I might go in later? Is that all right?'

'Sure. That's fine. Any time you want to go in Barry, we're right to go.'

I stood and moved to the doorway into the viewing room. Barry appeared to be tentative which is normal. I opened the door and I walked in first, keeping the door open as I allowed him to walk past me. From the doorway, he could see the body on the trolley. He froze as if unwilling to take the remaining steps to be close to the trolley.

'Take your time, Barry. No rush,' I said softly. He took one step and then another. He turned back towards me and looked into my eyes. 'Yes, that's him. It's definitely him.' Barry walked past me and back into the anteroom.

I noticed over the years how many men would do the same thing. They walk in, have a look from as far away as possible and then turn and walk out of there as quickly as possible.

A tragic crash; a young widow's nightmare

Women did the opposite. They walk in and approach the body and often caress, touch the hair, kiss and talk to the body. This wasn't always the case but women on the whole were far more hands on than the men; perhaps it is their way of dealing with these final moments with someone they love. I haven't come up with a comprehensive reason but I would venture that women are often more demonstrative than men and are more accustomed to displaying their emotions more openly than men, even in this most troubling time of bereavement. 'It's him Shaz, it's him.' I heard Barry in the anteroom telling Sharon what he had witnessed. 'I don't think you should see him, darling. It's not good for you,' Barry counselled.

I countered. 'It's like we said before Barry. I think Sharon has to make up her own mind. If she chooses to go in, that's fine. If she doesn't, that's ok too.' I faced Sharon as I sat down opposite her. 'It's completely up to you. I know your dad has got nothing but the best intentions for you, but I think it's up to you.'

'Dad, I think I'd like to see him.' The words were calm, definite. She was clear in what she wanted.

'But darling, it's just that I think you don't need to do this. What if you have an attack?' said Barry sounding desperate.

'Attack? What do you mean?' This was news to me. What

Chapter 9

did attack mean? Heart attack? Did Sharon have some sort of heart condition?

'Sorry. But what do you mean by attack? Do you have some sort of medical condition that I don't know about? If it's serious, I'd like to know before any final decision is made.'

'I've got epilepsy. I take medication for it. I get occasional fits. That's what Dad's talking about. He's just worried that I might fit and I could get hurt. It's all right, Dad. I can do this. I really want to do this. I need to see him. I know you don't like it Dad, but I'm his wife and I need to do this not just for me but for the kids too.' Sharon sounded just as definite as before, maybe more so. I could see Barry struggling for a reply but he looked at her and then just shrugged his shoulders. He knew when he was beaten.

'Ok, love. Do what you think is right.' He sounded resigned. He reached over and squeezed her hand. She looked at him and smiled.

'Thanks, Dad. I just want you to understand, that's all.' She turned to face me again. ' Will you come in with me, John. I'd like you to come too. Is that ok? You know, just in case I get scared. I think Dad can stay here. Is that ok, Dad?'

'Sure love, that's fine.' I think Barry looked somewhat relieved. He didn't look as though he wanted to go in the viewing room again. He leant back in the chair, as if to

A tragic crash; a young widow's nightmare

distance himself from the viewing.

'Whenever you're ready, we can go in. Do you have any more questions for me before we do? Anything you want me to clarify?' I asked gently.

'No. Let's go.' She stood and walked towards the viewing room door staying as close to me as she could get. I opened the door slowly and allowed her to walk past me ever so slowly. She stopped, as if frozen, turned away and held me.

'I'm scared,' she whispered. 'I don't want to believe it's him. I'm hoping that it isn't and it's all been a mistake.' She peered at him again. She sighed. 'But I can see it's him. Oh Charlie! Oh Charlie. Why?'

She took a few tentative steps towards him and then she was right alongside him, stroking his hair and bending down to kiss his forehead. 'Oh,' she withdrew her hand sharply, turning to face me. 'He is cold like you said. Oh, he feels so cold. Oh, my Charlie …' She turned again and resumed caressing and kissing him on the face.

I stood towards the back of the room, watching her. I'd seen hundreds of people over the years in the same place, whispering words of love and feeling the anguish. Crying, then turning to talk, maybe to ask a question. Often, I would walk forward, encouraging the person to touch or embrace, to say something to the dead, trying to make it a meaningful

Chapter 9

experience for them. Grief is a savage mistress. It will hurt you deeply; leaving scars that may never fully heal. I knew this was to be the start of a long and difficult journey for Sharon, one that can take years.

Sharon turned to me. 'Do you think he suffered?' she asked through her tears. 'I just don't want to think he suffered.'

'I don't think he did. He appears to have really bad chest injuries and I noticed a bad bump on his head and the lacerations on his face mean that he could easily have been knocked unconscious when the car hit the truck. I can let you know more when they do the autopsy. That will possibly be done tomorrow. I can call you after if you like and I let you know the results.'

'Thanks.' She turned back to her husband. Sharon spent half an hour talking, touching, kissing him, grieving. I stayed at my position at the back of the room, making sure she would be all right. She turned and looked at me. 'I'm ready to go. I think I'll leave now and go home to see the girls. I'm not sure what to tell them. Now they have no daddy.' She turned and touched his hand again. 'See you, darling. I love you.' She put her two fingers to her lips, kissed them and slowly placed them on his cold lips. 'Bye, my love.' She walked to me, smiled and with one last look at him went into the anteroom.

A tragic crash; a young widow's nightmare

Barry stood immediately. 'Are you all right, love?'

'Yes, Dad, I'm fine. I needed to do that. He's at peace now. He hasn't got any more worries.' She sat and I joined her, sitting opposite.

'Can I ask you a question please, Sharon?' I needed to know what she meant when she spoke of the girls. Did she have kids? She must have kids because she mentioned daddy. Sharon nodded. 'You mentioned girls in the viewing room. Do you have kids, Sharon?'

She nodded. 'Yes, two girls, Kayla and Tianne. Kayla's the oldest, she's four, and Tianne's just turned two. I don't know what I'm going to tell them. I know that Kayla will miss her daddy but Tianne's a bit young. What will I tell them?'

I spent the next half hour talking to Sharon about her kids. I explained to her that it was really important to be honest with them. Naturally, the two year old would have difficulties understanding the situation, but it was important that she be told the truth in an age-appropriate way. The four year old would have trouble understanding as well but less so than the younger daughter. I gave Sharon some names of useful books about explaining death to children and explained to her that kids can be and should be told the truth. Kids may not understand much about death and permanency but long term, they always remember that you

Chapter 9

told them the truth. The truth enables children to trust the parent in the long term. They would always be aware that mum told them the truth and did not lie to them about something so vital. Trust is always such an important factor in raising kids. Trust allows the child to develop and, in turn, to trust others, thus developing healthy relationships. When trust is shattered early, it becomes more difficult to develop trusting relationships later in life.

Sharon left with Barry. I was left with the feeling that Sharon needed access to regular support and counselling. It was going to be hard for her and for her children. I spoke with Sharon after the autopsy had been completed. I explained to her the injuries he received and after a conversation with the forensic pathologist, I reassured her that Charlie hadn't suffered as he became unconscious on impact. Sharon was relieved to hear this. She asked me whether we could tell more about the accident, what exactly had happened and what had caused the car to veer to the wrong side of the road in such a dramatic fashion. I told her we had no explanation for the accident. The car appeared to be in perfect working order according to the vehicle examination. I asked her if she could think of any explanation. Sharon was initially hesitant but then she went on to say that Charlie had a gambling habit and that recently he had lost large sums on

A tragic crash; a young widow's nightmare

poker machines. He had begun to gamble extensively and regularly lost thousands of dollars. The day of the accident he had lost much of his pay that he had received the day before. I wondered whether the accident was no accident but a deliberate act. I didn't mention it at the time, waiting for her to raise it if she ever felt the need.

Sharon came for counselling regularly. She initially attended once a fortnight but then it went to once a month. During the sessions, we spoke about how she was dealing with Charlie's death, how she was coping with being a single parent. Like most people, she cried and said that she was unsure about handling her kids. Sharon came to talk about how she felt and I reassured her on many occasions how feelings of anxiety and doubt are very normal. I was pleased to hear that she found our sessions very comforting. It was always Barry who dropped her off, heading off for a coffee while we spoke. Then one day she came in to see me out of the blue.

'John, I've been thinking a lot about Charlie since I last saw you. I've been thinking about the accident. But you know what? I'm really shitty with Charlie. I reckon he deliberately crashed the car 'cos he was scared that he lost so much money. I reckon he was just too scared to face me and the kids. He'd lost the money and he just couldn't bear it any

Chapter 9

more so I think he crashed on purpose to get out of it.' It all came out in a burst. She then looked at me hard. 'Well, tell me I'm wrong,' she said challengingly.

'I don't know if you're right or not. What you say makes sense and I have considered that before now. When you told me of his gambling habits and how much he had lost, I thought about how people can sometimes make bad decisions and want to end their lives. I know it's happened before. But, I don't know if you're right. The only person who knows the truth isn't here any more. Charlie's gone and we can't work out what he thought and what he wanted to do. You've thought a lot about it the last few weeks. What do you think it means if he did do it deliberately?'

'It means he's a cowardly shit. I'm really cranky with him and if he was here, I'd kill him, even though he's gone. How could he do that to the girls? They're still babies and they have to grow up without a father. That sucks. No, he's selfish. He shouldn't have done it.' She stopped and then bowed her head. 'But I still love him and I miss him still. How long does it take to stop missing someone, especially at night? I miss him coming home and giving the girls a bath, putting them to bed. Then we would watch telly. After they were in bed, he'd go outside to sneak a cigarette. I miss all the things he did. I loved him. Will I ever get that again, John?'

A tragic crash; a young widow's nightmare

'I don't know. It's been how long now, ten months? Often the first year is the hardest, given that you have to go through all the significant dates without him; birthdays, the first Christmas, the first Mothers' Day, the first Fathers' Day, anniversaries, all those things that you celebrated together. The first year without him is really hard. The anniversary of the death is coming up too. That sometimes is a really difficult time as well. You might find yourself thinking a lot about him in the next couple of months and sometimes the anniversary of his death is tough. It depends. Sometimes the time leading up can be harder than the actual day. It's really an individual thing. Not all people are the same. Just don't think you're crazy if you're finding it tough over the next couple of months.'

Leading up to the anniversary Sharon told me she had quite vivid dreams of Charlie. She told me she had dreams where he came back, dreams where she told him off for leaving her and the kids, dreams where she and Charlie were making love. After the anniversary passed, Sharon told me that the day had passed by without too much difficulty. She said she must have done all the work beforehand. Sharon jokingly told me she would give me a break for a few months. She didn't call for about six months and then one day I had a call from her. She asked if she could come and see me for a chat.

Chapter 9

I greeted her and she embraced me. 'It's good to see you,' I said. 'You look great. It's been a while. How have you been?'

'Really well. I just wanted your advice about something. You might laugh but I need some counselling about boys.' She giggled. I smiled. 'Yes, boys. There's a guy I like and I want to know whether I'm doing the right thing. Is it normal to like a guy when it's not even two years since Charlie died? Am I weird for fancying a guy so soon? I guess I want to know, am I normal?' She laughed. 'And don't say I'm weird again, John. I know I am.' She was clearly in a good mood and I could sense that she wanted reassurance.

'Of course, you're normal. I think it's fabulous that you like this guy. It is one guy, not twelve?' She laughed as I teased her.

'Yes, of course it's normal. You like this guy. How much more normal can you get? Does he like you?' I quizzed.

'Yes, I think so. We've been dating for about two months and I really like him and he really likes me. He's been to my home and he loves the girls too. He's one of Charlie's old friends and we've known each other for years. I never thought we would be anything but friends but he's been so good at listening and we've just become closer and closer. It's just been great. I just really like being around him. He's smart and funny and he makes me laugh. He's unreal. You

A tragic crash; a young widow's nightmare

know what I mean?' She smiled a beaming smile. She looked genuinely happy. I was pleased for her. To find someone is hard and clearly she had found someone that she really liked. We spoke about the relationship for the rest of the session. She beamed and joked as she told me stories about her new beau, Michael. I was happy for her.

She rang me six months later to tell me that they had decided to get married. She sounded thrilled and told me I was invited. I declined the kind invitation as I explained that counsellors don't usually attend their client's weddings. She understood and thanked me for all the work I had done. She told me she wouldn't have survived without my help. I appreciated what she said and wished her all the best for the future. I told her to call me if she ever needs to talk. I didn't see her for another six months.

I was at my desk one afternoon when one of the clerical staff called me and told me a woman was at the front desk by the name of Sharon. I immediately went out to greet her, pleased she had dropped in to see me. I opened the door into the foyer and saw Sharon standing with her dad, Barry. She was in tears and Barry looked very anxious. 'Sharon, what's wrong?'

'It's Michael. He's dead. Oh John, what am I going to do? It's happened again.' She held onto me as she wept, her

Chapter 9

shoulders heaving.

'Sharon, come through and we'll talk.' She told me that Michael had died of a drug overdose. Evidently, he was a recreational user according to Sharon and he died accidentally from a combination of drugs. He had just been taken to the morgue and Sharon had arrived soon after. She knew I was working in a different section of the Coroner's Court but had come straight to me. I was saddened to hear her news. It was shocking to think that two partners had died unexpectedly in two years.

Because of my changed circumstances, I had to refer her to another counsellor at Glebe. I didn't find out how this worked out but I found her very resilient and hoped that she would cope with this new loss.

I have occasionally thought about Sharon and wondered how she survived being a widow twice before the age of thirty. To lose one partner is hard enough, to lose two in quick succession is almost too much to contemplate.

CHAPTER 10

THE BALI BOMBINGS

I did a job once that involved the repatriation of the dead.

I had recently moved jobs when the Bali bombings happened on 12 October 2002. I had just taken a position within the Office of the NSW State Coroner as the Head of the Coronial Information and Support Program. I was no longer involved in the forensic side of things but my task was to liaise with the Department of Foreign Affairs and Trade, the Federal Police and Forensic Medical teams to ensure the proper repatriation of the dead into Australia. This was probably the hardest job I have ever done.

The bombings, carried out by a violent Islamic extremist group, were planned to coincide with one of the busiest tourist times at Kuta Beach when many Australian sporting teams are in Kuta on their annual end-of-season break. The first bomb was detonated by a suicide bomber inside

Chapter 10

the popular nightclub, Paddy's Irish Bar causing a fire to break out. Many patrons, some of whom were badly burned, escaped into the street. Twenty seconds later, across the road of the same street, a second and much more deadly car bomb, hidden inside a van, was detonated outside the Sari Club, an open-air, thatched-roof bar opposite Paddy's bar. A metre-wide crater was all that was left where the van had been. The number of people dead and injured overwhelmed the local medical and hospital facilities. The third bomb outside the US Embassy in Denpasar caused only minor damage.

The bombs in the main street of Kuta killed 202 people, many of whom were Balinese. Eighty-eight Australians were among the dead. In response, a Disaster Victim Identification team was sent from Australia including a number of people I knew well. It was an extremely challenging task for the team that included professionals from all over Australia who worked alongside many Indonesian specialists. There was significant pressure from families of the deceased to have their loved one's body released as soon as possible. Some family members genuinely felt they had visually identified their loved one only to be told that it was a different person. Dental examination, fingerprinting and DNA testing were the methods used to identify the dead. Visual identification was impossible in many cases as the bodies were fragmented

The Bali bombings

and badly burnt. I can understand people wanting to believe they had correctly identified their family member but the bodies required absolute, undeniable identification before they could be released. The release of the wrong person to a family was not a consideration so, to ensure this didn't happen, the families had to wait despite the extra anguish and distress this may cause. The identification process for this incident was unprecedented in recent times – the numbers of bodies, the state of them which made identification difficult and that the bodies needed to be repatriated to Australia – meant that families had to wait.

In terms of identification, there were local issues in Bali that were a cause of some concern. Bali has a tropical climate and the extreme heat was a factor. Naturally, bodies deteriorate quicker when exposed to higher temperatures. To ease the crisis, five refrigerated containers capable of handling up to 17 bodies each were flown in by the RAAF. Workers at the local morgue had to use slabs of ice to help prevent bodies from decomposing in the overworked, makeshift morgue. How to manage the storage and identification of bodies was a major challenge faced by the team in Bali.

The state coroners from two Australian states went to Bali to advise on the identification and repatriation process. I was told my task would be to liaise with the Federal Government

Chapter 10

and non-government agencies to ensure families were notified and could be present when the body of their family member was returned to Australia. I attended a series of meetings with the Federal Police, the Sydney Airport Authority and the Department of Foreign Affairs and Trade (DFAT). All were very keen to assist in what was a complex and difficult task. I had received a series of telephone calls from Bali about the process they were following and I was clear about my role.

I was to keep in touch with the families, to advise them that it was going to be a slow process and to ask them to be patient. We needed to make sure that the right person was returned to the right family. Due to the large numbers of bodies involved, I needed to let families know that it could take weeks. I was to be involved in receiving information from Bali, detailing each person's remains. I would then arrange to meet the families at Sydney airport and ensure that the remains were taken back to the Glebe morgue. Following this, each family could arrange a funeral director to collect the body for cremation or burial.

The decision to have the families greet the deceased at the airport was a curious one. Certainly, it is customary that the bodies of those who die overseas on military service are met by family members and other dignitaries. The decision

The Bali bombings

to have families greet the bodies from Bali was made by someone at DFAT. From the reactions of the families I met, the decision appears to have been a good one.

I received news that the first remains were due to arrive in Sydney. I was in touch with the Sydney Airports Authority and they were excellent in advising what would happen. We were all to meet in rooms at the freight arrival section of the airport. I remember driving to the International Airport, anxious to make sure that the arrival went without fuss. I had never been to this area before and as I arrived, I was ushered through into one of the rooms at the freight terminal. Already present were members of DFAT. I greeted them and spoke with some of the QANTAS staff present. All of us were anxious that events would go smoothly. A family arrived and we all introduced each other. I explained the steps in the process as best as I could and apologised for the delays. The family accepted the need for accuracy over speed. I was interrupted by a staff member.

'Sorry John. The container has just been unloaded. Can you come and take a look and make sure everything is good before we let the family come in?' I walked through a series of doors before arriving in what looked like a warehouse. There was a large container and inside was a large metallic coffin-like box. A woman had followed me from Foreign

Chapter 10

Affairs and she looked at the box.

'Now what we will do is place an Australian flag on top of the coffin. We can then allow the family to come and pay their respects. What do you think, John?'

This is part of the procedure for Australian servicemen and women who have died overseas: the coffins are always draped in the national flag. I agreed without much thought. 'Yeah, I think that would be good. It might take away a little from the harshness of the box. It also shows respect and recognises they are Australian. I think that's a really good idea.'

The flag was duly placed on top of the coffin and we allowed the family to enter. They came and stood around it. Some cried, others stood stoically. The flag seemed to mean so much to them. I was grateful that the woman had come up with such a good idea. I left the warehouse and spoke with the funeral director who would take the coffin back to Glebe. Naturally, I knew the guys.

'Hi John. How's things going in there?' A man I had known for years was the funeral director. He was a man who had conducted many funerals, and was a thoroughly decent man.

'All good. Hey tell me, are you going to page in front of the hearse?' This is the term used to describe the walk of the

The Bali bombings

undertaker in front of the hearse at a funeral. In older times, the hearse was drawn by horses and the walk was used to moderate the speed of the horses. I'm sure many have seen the sight of a person walking in front of a hearse. It's a sign of respect and I considered the family would be pleased to witness this formality.

'Of course,' he responded. 'I thought that would be the best we could do given the tragic circumstances.' He sounded very earnest and anxious to do the right thing for the family. I thanked him and walked back into the warehouse area.

I spoke with the family members and suggested that the family walk alongside the coffin as it was wheeled out into the bright sunlight through a large door. The coffin, mounted on a trolley, made its way out of the building with family members walking alongside. The funeral director waited, his stance respectful and formal. He nodded to the family, extending his hand in greeting. The senior family member shook his hand, thanking him for his work. The coffin was loaded into the hearse and the door shut. The funeral director then commenced his walk in front of the hearse until the gate where he solemnly stopped and waited for the hearse to pull up alongside. He climbed into the passenger seat and the hearse slowly drove away and out of sight.

Chapter 10

There were some employees working in their regular day jobs around the area. All stood, sombre, heads bowed out of respect, hands either behind their backs or clasped in front of them. It was very moving. Some of the staff were crying softly and were visibly distressed. It was as if they were welcoming home a fallen soldier, someone who had fallen on foreign soil and was being brought back to his family. A large man, in his late forties, in a high visibility vest watched the sombre procession. He raised his right hand slowly in a salute. Respect for a fallen soul.

Once the hearse had disappeared, the family shook our hands and embraced some of the tearful staff. I didn't shed a tear. I was always mindful of my role in any proceedings such as these. I couldn't let my emotions interfere with the professional service I was providing. I often had felt like crying at numerous viewings and at different times in the course of my work but had succumbed only once.

On this occasion, I was the only member of the coronial team present. Usually we work in a team, often comprised of fellow counsellors or other team members from the assistants or the forensic pathologists. We understand each other's roles and are able to support each other. On this day, working solo, it was one of the few times in my career that I felt a general sense of being isolated. It didn't affect the

The Bali bombings

work I did nor did it diminish the role I played but I didn't enjoy the feeling. I wanted someone there to be part of this, to understand and witness these events with me. I wanted to share this tale with at least one other colleague, to get their opinion, witness their reaction to it all. That was not to be; I was alone.

I looked around at the group that was beginning to disperse. The DFAT staff walked to their vehicles, the other staff went back to their duties, some embracing and comforting each other. I got the sense that no one felt terribly comfortable around me. I drove back to Glebe. The hearse had only arrived minutes before me. I saw the family in the foyer. I went upstairs to the coroner to let him know that things had gone well. I spoke to him, explaining what we had done, the flag, the procession; everything had gone smoothly.

I received another message from Bali. More body parts were being returned. The message outlined what body parts were coming in and to whom they belonged. The message went into some detail. It said something like: left clavicle, right femur, left tibia, skull, jaw. It was very specific. The body parts were listed as separate items. In a bomb blast such as Bali, bodies are badly mutilated; often only parts of the body are left to be identified. We are all aware of this, but to

Chapter 10

see it written in such specific, medical detail was confronting for families who were always informed what body parts were being returned. Contact was made with them and details of the flight were given.

I received a call from Sydney airport late one afternoon. The second arrival was due the next morning. I had already received confirmation of the body parts from Bali. I headed off in the morning and, once again, arrived at the freight terminal. I usually arrived early so I could liaise with the relevant authorities before seeing the family and tending to the coffin. As I arrived I saw the family waiting at their car. I recognised them from the numerous media photographs and television interviews that had been done. I wandered across to them and introduced myself.

'Hi, I'm John from the Coroner's office,' I smiled in greeting.

'Hi. Yes we know who you are,' said a man. 'You people have delayed everything. We identified him back in Bali and you've dragged this out for ages. What takes so long? I saw him the day after it happened. I spoke with the cops over there and they said he would be released quickly. How long does this thing take? I'm sick of all this bullshit bureaucratic red tape. Sorry mate, but we're over it. We came today to make sure there are no more delays. Can't you see we're the

The Bali bombings

victims here? I'm sure you guys don't care. You just want to do all the testing and it's killing his mother. She's not here today. She's back at home waiting to hear from us when he gets in. I identified him, me. I'm sure it was my son. Now you're saying I'm wrong ...' He ran out of things to say. He was shaking with anger.

I was aware that some of family members of different victims of the bombing had tried to visually identify their loved ones in Bali. They had seen the body and thought that they had identified the body as their relative. Often this had been done supervised by a kind-natured individual, anxious to help a distressed family. It had been done for all the right compassionate reasons. However, I had been told by one of the team in Bali that nine people had been visually identified incorrectly. Psychologically, I can understand the desire to recognise someone you love. I can understand the desperation one must feel in wanting to believe that you have seen your relative. I knew that this man was one of the family members who had flown to Bali and had incorrectly identified his relative. Further testing proved that the visual identification was incorrect. I could feel the man's anguish and frustration and could tell he was angry that the process had been so lengthy.

'I am really sorry ...,' I began.

Chapter 10

The man snorted in derision 'You're sorry. I told you I saw him in Bali. I saw him. I was told he'd be released quickly. Don't tell me you're sorry. You tell the coroner that we're going to take this matter further. I'll speak to the media …' Again he seemed to run out of words.

'Like I said, I'm very sorry for the length of time this process is taking. I am sorry for the stress on your family. It must be really hard for you all. I just want to explain a few things to you about what happened and about the whole ID process.' I tried to diffuse the confrontation, apologise for the time involved and avoid a further escalation of the situation.

'No mate, don't start with explanations. Like I said before, we're over it. Enough's enough.' He turned away from me as if in disgust.

'You know what, mate,' I said, 'you identified the wrong person. You wanted to believe it was him but you were wrong. You thought it was him because you saw someone who looked like him. I spoke with the forensic team in Bali. The bloke you identified is another man, a different man altogether. We have now identified him correctly. Yes, we have taken a long time doing it. I accept that. But you know what? I want to make sure you get the right person back to bury. I want to make sure every family, not just yours, gets

The Bali bombings

the right person back. That's what I want. I want to be sure. We won't accept maybes or possibilities. We want certainty. We are doing this for all the families. That's the truth here. Get shitty with me all you like, but I'm not shying away from making sure we do the right thing for everyone.'

I was breathing hard and I had raised my voice to him. I noticed the rest of the family were looking at me in a state of mild shock. Some early morning workers had stopped and stared at the tone of my voice. Oh God, I thought, I've yelled at a bereaved family. What the hell have I done? I looked at the man who had turned and faced me during my rant. He looked hard into my eyes and I could recognise the pain. He said nothing for a few seconds. His face dropped and he looked down.

'Oh, I am so sorry for raising my voice. I am …' It was my turn to run out of words. I didn't know what to say. I felt a complete bastard. He had every right to feel angry, every right to feel upset at the perceived inadequacies in the system, angry that his son had been taken from him. I had no right to be angry. I should have shut the hell up.

Then he spoke again. 'No,' he said raising his head and looking at me. 'You're right. I didn't realise that I identified the wrong bloke. I thought it was my son. I thought that it was just red tape that was slowing things down. I forgot that

Chapter 10

other families are going through what we are going through. No, you're right. I just thought … doesn't matter now.'

He sounded deflated, resigned but he was no longer angry. The other family members gathered around him, clasping his shoulder, others embracing him. He turned back to me after a few minutes. I stood there half expecting him to reawaken in anger. He held out his hand.

'Nice to meet you, John. You know for a counsellor, you're pretty fuckin' cranky. Thanks for your honesty. I'm pleased that the Coroner's office has got someone like you riding shotgun.' He smiled and I shook his hand warmly.

'I'm not usually this cranky. I'm usually worse.'

He laughed. 'Come on in and we can talk more as we wait for his arrival. Ok?'

We walked through the gate and met with the DFAT staff and the usual welcoming staff from QANTAS. I moved away from the family as they were quickly surrounded by attentive and caring teams from all sides. Soon after, I was told that the flight had landed. I went to the warehouse and the staff had already placed the flag on the coffin and it was awaiting the family.

As had happened with the first coffin from Bali, this one was placed on a trolley being wheeled out through the large door, followed by family, staff standing to attention to show

The Bali bombings

respect. There were many who watched the procession, some in tears.

It was a sight to which I quickly became accustomed. I would stand to one side and witness the grief of the family, the tears of strangers, and the slow departure of the hearse.

More calls came, more arrivals, more scenes at the freight terminal. Occasionally, families did not wish to greet the coffin. Some valued privacy and preferred to be alone with their deceased loved one; others did not see any benefit of attending at the airport. Whatever the circumstances, I went anyway. I wanted to ensure that the same procedure was followed, that each body received the same welcome home. I wanted to see everyone treated equally.

Some families wished to have the cremations held in Sydney and their ashes returned to their rural homes. I agreed to organise these services and return the ashes personally. I had spoken on the phone with country families and felt duty bound to ensure the safe return of the ashes to them wherever they lived in the state.

I went to the crematorium one day to collect the ashes of someone who had died in the bombings. I drove the winding road through the cemetery to the light brick offices of the crematorium, collected the plastic box and placed it in the boot of the car. I drove for hours westward to the

Chapter 10

home of the family, stayed overnight in the country town then returned to Sydney the next day.

I had time on my hands as I drove out. It was unusual to have so much time to reflect on this dreadful mass killing that had taken so many lives. It gave me time to also reflect on my job in general; what I do, why I do it and what it means to me.

As I drove through the countryside, I thought about all these things. Yes, I thought, I'm doing the right thing. The family asked me to sort this for them and that's what I am doing. I thought back to the hours I had spent at the freight terminal in Sydney. I thought of the mourners, the strangers crying, the teams of staff visibly moved by the experience. I could picture in my mind the staff crying, the family members devastated at the loss of their loved one. I had embraced people and comforted them in their loss. I had listened to them as they shared stories about their relative who had perished, their feelings of loss at the sudden heart-wrenching devastation. But I wondered why, unlike many of the people who did not know the victims and who had been moved to tears, why I didn't cry. Sure, I am a professional counsellor and we are conditioned not to get involved personally. How was I seemingly unaffected by what I saw and did, not only at the airport, but also in my

The Bali bombings

work generally? As I drove on, I felt a hollowness inside. Maybe that's what happens to people sometimes. There's something called compassion fatigue, burnout, secondary traumatisation. I decided that when I returned, I would have a chat to one of my colleagues. We are a tight team, often in each other's offices talking about cases, sharing stories, laughing, supporting each other. For this particular job meeting the bodies and families at the airport, I missed that camaraderie and I would make sure I develop it again. But first, the delivery of these ashes was the order of the day.

I found the family home, on the outskirts of a regional town. I met the family, lovely caring people, and stayed for a coffee but not for long. I went to the motel that I had booked for the night and went straight to the bar. I spent the next two hours drinking and occasionally talking to the barmaid. She had assumed I was a travelling salesman or marketing person. I let her believe what she wanted to believe. I didn't want to talk about the reasons I was there. At one stage, she spoke about her friends in town. She looked bored and I was the only one drinking at the time. She chatted away about the town and things in general. She stood opposite me behind the bar and faced me.

'You know the Bali bombings?' she asked. I nodded in response. 'Yeah, not much though,' I lied.

Chapter 10

'I lost a mate over there. I went to school with him and I know his family real well. They're doing it tough. It's been weeks waiting for him to be returned back here. There's a bloke coming today from Sydney whose bringing back some of my friend's ashes. We're going around there tomorrow for a ceremony at his folk's place.' She wiped the bar for the hundredth time. Then she went on.

'It's so hard for his mum. She's not been the same since it happened. Oh, sorry to bring this up with you. You probably just want to have a quiet drink and here's me going on.'

'No, it's fine. It must be hard for his mum and all his family. So you said there's going to be a ceremony, is there. What's that about?'

'They're going to have all his mates attend and they're going to place the ashes somewhere, or sprinkle them. I'm not sure. We'll just get together and talk about him, have a few drinks to his memory, you know.'

'Sounds like it's going to be a really worthwhile thing to do for his family. I think it's great that his mum's got people like you around to help her at the moment. Hope it goes well tomorrow.'

'Thanks. I don't know why I brought it up. Sorry if it was a downer for you. It's easy talking to you. I can see you'd be good at doing sales. Maybe you missed your chance,' she

The Bali bombings

laughed out loud. 'Maybe you should have been a counsellor. You'd do all right at that.' She laughed again. 'Another one for you, same again?' she asked.

'No thanks. I've had enough. I'll grab dinner later and maybe come back for a drink afterwards. Cheers.' With that, I walked away. Yeah, I thought, maybe I could be a counsellor one day. One day, but not this day.

I rang Helen after dinner. I told her I missed her and loved her. She understood I was feeling lonely. She could tell in my voice. She told me everything was fine at home and chided me gently about being away. I knew what she meant. I crawled into bed later that evening. I had drunk too much wine and I just wanted to sleep. Trucks rumbled by along the highway keeping me from a deep sleep. I thought about the barmaid and the family and of the ceremony they would be holding tomorrow. I hoped things work out well tomorrow. I wasn't even sure what I meant by that but I wanted them to feel a sense of comfort; that they had finally laid their son to rest at home. The barmaid was the sort of friend people needed. She would hopefully help the family out during this most difficult of times.

I can't remember feeling so alone than during the work on the Bali bombings. This sounds incredibly selfish. Here I am moaning about me when so many people's lives were lost in

Chapter 10

a terrorist bombing and many more affected by the deaths. Their loved ones had gone away on what should have been a fun-filled holiday, bringing back stories of their time in Bali. Instead, they had come back in body bags.

   I had no right to feel this way. I felt alienated from my team and disconnected from my current colleagues. I should have done what I thought on that trip west and spoken to someone. I didn't. I hardly spoke to anyone about what I was doing on this job. I now realise the mistake I made. I had been more affected by this work than I originally thought. I started to think that it might be time to move on; to have a break. I began to look for jobs in other areas. An opportunity for a secondment arose. The job was an investigator at the Health Care Complaints Commission. I received permission to take a secondment there for twelve months and applied. When I was found out that I had the job, my heart leaped with excitement. It's not that I wanted to leave. I just needed a break.

CHAPTER 11

EXPECT THE UNEXPECTED AT AN INQUEST

I did a job once where I travelled the state to go to inquests.

After my work helping to repatriate the dead from the Bali bombing, I needed a break from the morgue and took a secondment at the Health Care Commission for twelve months. After one year there, I was pleased to be returning to the Coroner's office.

My colleagues and friends welcomed me warmly on my return. It somehow felt right to be back, back to where I belonged.

I arrived at the office to find little had changed in many ways. Maybe the break had done me some good. The constant barrage of death and dealing with grieving families had ceased for the twelve months I was at the commission.

Chapter 11

My own family had had their own bereavement with the death of my eldest brother from a brain tumour and my colleagues at the commission had been very supportive. My time there was spent investigating various complaints against health professionals. I decided looking into 'naughty nurses' and 'dirty doctors' best described the work I had been doing. Strangely, after about seven months, I was looking forward to getting back to the morgue and helping families in their grief. I felt that the secondment was necessary to give me some breathing space without actually having to leave. And it was good to be back; there were still some things I wanted to do at the Coroner's office.

Back in the saddle, I hit the ground running keen to develop new ideas and new programs. I began to focus more on witness and family support during the formal court process known as an inquest. These are held at Glebe in Sydney but also in towns and cities around New South Wales. Country inquests take time. Those from the Coroner's Court would often travel together by road, stay as long as necessary to complete the proceedings and travel home.

As previously mentioned, the coroner has to determine several things – the identity of the deceased, the time and place of death and the cause and manner of death. The coroner holds an inquest when one or more of these factors

Expect the unexpected at an inquest

is uncertain or when the Coroner's Court is legally bound to hold an inquest. An inquest is also held in the case of an unsolved homicide and may also be held in cases where there is substantial public interest or there is a need to examine systems that may have contributed to a death. This last instance was the case when Phillip Hughes died on the cricket pitch of the Sydney Cricket Ground on 24 November 2014 after being struck by a ball in the side of his head. The inquest into Hughes' death was held to determine if there were any circumstances contributing to his death that could have been avoided. And Phillip Hughes' death is one that certainly met the criteria for a 'public interest' inquest.

An inquest is held in a formal setting. A magistrate, as coroner, sits behind a bench at the front of the court and is assisted by someone who asks questions on the coroner's behalf. This person is either a police officer acting as Sergeant Assisting the Coroner or Counsel Assisting – a legal officer, often a barrister, with extensive experience. In some matters, a police sergeant assists the coroner and in more high profile complex matters, Counsel Assisting is used. The coroner listens to the evidence and determines, on the balance of probabilities, the identity, time, place, cause and manner of death.

A brief of evidence is collated by the investigating police

Chapter 11

and submitted to the coroner. Witnesses are called and have to testify under oath. It is a court in every sense of the word but no judgements are made against people. Coroners don't determine guilt or innocence. As such people do not have the opportunity to defend themselves in the Coroner's Court. A coroner's verdict can be natural death, accidental death, death by misadventure, suicide or murder, to name a few. If the verdict is murder or if someone is found to be culpable for a death, criminal prosecution may follow, and suspects are able to defend themselves against any case brought in a different court. A coroner can only refer matters to the Public Prosecution office for this to happen.

Even though a coroner cannot bring any action against person or persons, it is often a dramatic and worrying time for witnesses and family members unused to court proceedings. For this reason, the coroner may try to create a welcoming atmosphere in an attempt to help family and others to be more relaxed, a feat easier said than done.

People can be nervous and often rather tongue-tied when in the Coroner's Court. I sat in on numerous inquests where the coroner would try to soothe the family by speaking with them from behind the bench. At one inquest the coroner left the bench and walked into court, warmly embracing the family and shaking people's hands. It was a genuine

Expect the unexpected at an inquest

expression from the coroner involved and one that was welcomed by all who witnessed the incident.

So while the court proceedings are very similar to that of a magistrate's court, the coroner's court can be a little more relaxed too where humour plays a part. Here's what I mean.

The session in Coroner's Court was about to begin. 'Silence. All stand,' said the attendant as per normal courtroom procedure. The coroner entered and took her place behind the imposing bench. It was her turn to speak.

'Please, be seated. Good morning everyone. This is an inquest into the death of Mr John Smith. Counsel Assisting?'

'Good morning, Your Honour. Fiona Smith, Counsel for the Coroner.' The coroner nods.

'John Jones seeks leave to appear for Mr Bill Bloggs of the Meat Factory,' said the lawyer representing the Meat Factory at the inquest.

'Thank you, Mr Jones.' The coroner looked around the courtroom. 'Are there are any family members here today of Mr Bill Smith?' she added looking towards me. I was sitting next to Mr Smith senior, the father of the man who had died. I looked sideways at Mr Smith. He sat there not saying a word. I nudged him. 'That's you, Mr Smith,' I whispered.

Mr Smith turned and whispered back. 'You're not

Chapter 11

supposed to talk in court. That's what you said to me. You said not to speak unless told by the coroner. That's what you said.'

The coroner still had eyes on us. She waited.

'Look,' I whispered back. 'The coroner has asked you a question. She just wants to know if there is any family here. You can just say yes, and introduce yourself. Go on. Answer him.' I was whispering but, because of the silence in the room, it seemed much louder.

Mr Smith stood, a little nervous. 'My name is Smith, your Honour. I'm John's dad. Sorry I didn't talk earlier but I was told not to speak unless the coroner speaks to me… that's you, Your Honour. My mate here got me a bit confused. All good now. Thanks, Your Honour. Just wasn't sure. I'll sit down now, thank you.' Mr Smith sat. The coroner smiled a broad smile. The rest of the court giggled ever so slightly.

'Thank you, Mr Smith. I appreciate your attendance here today. We'll do what we can to get to all the facts surrounding your son's sad passing.'

• • •

On one occasion I was asked by the Deputy State Coroner to travel into the country for an inquest. The case was a terrible one where a little girl had been mauled to death by dogs that

Expect the unexpected at an inquest

had been bred to hunt feral pigs. The owners of the dogs were a father and son team. I cannot speak highly enough of these two men – decent, honest and hard-working. Both had been devastated when their dogs had savaged and killed the girl. The men had known the little girl very well and had been de-facto relations of the youngster. Naturally, there had been a great degree of public interest in the death and an inquest was held. I had not spoken to the two men before the inquest and I made myself known to them as soon as I arrived. They were clearly more at ease in the bush and not accustomed to wearing anything but jeans or shorts, work clothes and the like. The two men wore ties that clearly had been in their wardrobes for several decades and wore shirts that had no colour references to the ties. They looked ill at ease, to say the least.

I introduced myself to them both and spoke with them at length. I explained what the coroner wanted to know and what the rules in court would be. We spoke for some time, and I was impressed by their decency and humanity. They were good men and were obviously feeling the loss of the little girl greatly.

Both men took the stand, one after the other, and were very credible witnesses. They both spoke clearly and deliberately about the circumstances surrounding the death. Both looked

Chapter 11

exhausted at the end and were keen to be on their way. The coroner grabbed me and told me to tell the men they had a done a great job and they were to be commended for their honesty. I quickly went to the court foyer and approached the men.

'Sorry guys. The coroner wants to pass on a message.' They both looked immediately concerned.

'What did we do?' asked the father.

'It's not you, I said looking at the father. 'It's your son.' The coroner wants him charged for crimes against fashion,' I said earnestly.

It took a while to sink in then they both both burst into laughter. 'That coroner's a top person. If she ever wants a beer, she knows where we are. You're both welcome any time.' His son looked at me.

'This bloody tie, mate. Would you believe I've never worn one before today?'

'Really? You're kidding me, right.' I responded trying not to sound too sarcastic.

They both laughed again. I guess it was a release. They had been wound tight and now they could relax and go back to their lives. I went back to speak with the coroner and told her what had transpired. 'How do you get away with it?' she asked. 'How the hell do you get away with it?'

Expect the unexpected at an inquest

• • •

In 2007, we welcomed a new State Coroner, Mary Jerram, who was an intelligent, experienced magistrate. Her Honour was highly skilled and a shrewd operator. Not only did she possess great legal acumen, but she also had a wonderful sense of humour and we quickly developed a really great rapport. All in all, the team of State Coroners and Deputy State Coroners were a highly effective group, a team lead impeccably by Her Honour Magistrate Mary Jerram.

Her Honour and I travelled to the far north west of New South Wales for an inquest with a court officer; a quiet man who said little when he was in the office at Glebe. We flew into a large country town, picked up a hire car at the airport and drove the remaining distance into the bush. As we drove further into the outback, our court officer became more and more laconic, a typical outback bushman, his voice slowing noticeably as he began to speak more than I had ever heard before.

'Yep, you gotta' watch the bush chooks,' he said a lot slower than you're reading this. 'Yep, they can be a menace drivin' out here. You know sometimes they'll run alongside

Chapter 11

the car and suddenly, quick as a flash they bolt out in front of you. I've collected a few over the years,' he said in his best bush voice.

'What the hell is happening to you?' I blurted out. 'The more west we go, the more you sound like Crocodile Dundee.'

'Well, you can take the boy out of the country, but you can't …'

'Yeah, yeah, I get it,' I snorted. Mary laughed in the backseat.

A while later. 'Can we stop here for a minute. Just want to stretch my legs and have a cigarette,' I said. 'Ok with everyone?'

'Sure, John' said the officer I now thought of as Dundee. 'Just don't stray far from the road, will ya.'

I stepped out of the car, stretching and easing the knots in my back. I shrugged my shoulders and began to pace into the spiny grass area adjacent to the road. No cars passed. It seemed quiet.

'Just watch for snakes,' came Dundee's voice. 'There's heaps every square foot out here.'

I stepped very quickly out from the grass and onto the verge. 'What, snakes, here, near the road? For God's sake! Where have we come to? I'm surrounded by snakes and

Expect the unexpected at an inquest

being driven by Crocodile Dundee. I'm in the twilight zone.' Mary just laughed. We drove further and I noticed whenever a car or vehicle drove past us the other way, Dundee would lift his index finger from the steering wheel in some sort of salute to the other driver. Sure enough, all the drivers responded in kind, each lifting their finger ever so slightly in recognition of a fellow traveller. Always the index finger. I thought I would have to try that when I got a turn to drive.

The inquest itself was a sad tale. Deaths of young people in a motor vehicle accident always are. This time, police had been in pursuit of two young people who subsequently crashed and died. Because their deaths occurred during the police chase, an inquest was mandatory. I met with the families, each devastated by the loss of the young people. The inquest was in a small town and it was as hot as hell. Everyone sweltered in court. The fans spun slowly above us in a vain attempt to cool, succeeding only in pushing the hot air around the courtroom.

A young man was called to give evidence. A rather pompous barrister was asking him about his statement.

'Sir, I draw your attention to page three, paragraph four. In it you say you ...' he detailed something in a long-winded manner. 'Now Sir, would you kindly read paragraph three,

Chapter 11

page eight of your statement to the court. The young man looked down from the witness box. He looked upset. 'I realise this can be trying Sir, but I urge you to read page eight, paragraph three. Can you see that in front of you, Sir? Do you have a copy of your statement there, Sir?' he continued.

'He can't read.' a voice beside me whispered. 'He never learnt.' I looked at the woman beside me. Of course, this made sense.

I tried to mouth 'he can't read' to the coroner but couldn't get her attention. One of the barristers suddenly tweaked. He leant and whispered to the pompous one who looked a little shaken at the news. He looked around the court and appeared to be wondering where to go next. 'Sir, what I would like to do is to read the statement, well parts of it, and then I will ask you some questions about these parts. Do you understand, Sir?' The man nodded and looked a little less stressed.

'That's more like it,' said the voice next to me. She turned out to be his aunt, a lovely woman who had attended to make sure firstly that her nephew turned up and secondly to support him. We tend to forget that sometimes we assume a level of knowledge and skills. We forget that there are many in our society far less equipped to handle situations beyond their normal lives; those who are less resourced and often

Expect the unexpected at an inquest

live in poverty and trying circumstances.

The people I met at inquests were invariably decent, hard-working individuals. There was often talk of no jobs being available, no income in town and a feeling that the future was going to be hard. They were all concerned about the youngsters growing up. How would they live? What would they do?

Of course, what they do – because there isn't much else – is jump in their cars and go for a drive. It was the reason we were here. In this case, the police had chased the car of young people – with deadly consequences.

I took my turn at driving on the return journey. I remembered Dundee's finger motion and I was excited when a vehicle approached in the opposite direction. Here goes I thought. I raised my index finger in a friendly salute. Nothing! I must have done something wrong. I'll raise it a bit higher next time. Yeah, maybe it's the height, I thought. The next car came along. I raised my finger in salute. Nothing again. 'Hey Dundee, my finger wave isn't working. When you do it, they all reply. Why aren't they responding? What am I doing wrong?' I asked more in exasperation.

'Dunno,' came the reply. 'Maybe they know you're scared of snakes.' Mary laughed out loud.

Chapter 11

Attending inquests was something that many of the forensic counselling team had to do. My colleague, Maurice, attended many. He was a brilliant storyteller and a warm, compassionate human being. He had a quiet presence about him. He was measured in his speech but when he spoke, people listened. He was also one of the funniest men I have ever known.

He attended an inquest in the bush into an unsolved homicide with the coroner on one occasion. During the trip, a lawyer had appeared at this inquest who was renowned for being overly verbose. He had almost refused to listen to the answers provided by the witness. He kept on sailing through his questions, completely ignoring the answers. This was evident to most people in the courtroom.

On his return, Maurice was keen to tell us about the lawyer and his interaction with a witness. 'Honestly, this is what it was like,' as Maurice took to impersonating the lawyer and witness in question.

'Now Sir, if I can ask you to remember the night of the fourteenth of June. You drove your vehicle down Smith Street in a northerly direction. Is that so, witness Bloggs?'

'Yes, you have me on toast. I did it. I killed her. It was me.'

'Now Sir, You then travelled to John Street and travelled west. Is that correct, Sir.'

Expect the unexpected at an inquest

'Yep, I did it. You have me dead to rights.'

'So after you travelled from John Street, you saw the victim standing on the north west corner of Bay Street; I withdraw that Your Honour, the north west corner of Blay Street.'

'I can't make it plainer. I killed her and buried her out of town.'

'Now. When did you first see the victim on the corner?'

'Ummm, that I can't remember.'

We all laughed at the tale. Many of us had been witness to pompous lawyers in our time. Despite the fact we dealt with death every day, there was still an opportunity to laugh, to rid ourselves of some of the negativity surrounding the investigations into death. Maurice no doubt had the capacity to provide some light relief. We found a sense of comfort when we had the chance to just sit around telling stories that would be too horrible for those who don't work at the morgue. The laughter helped us cope with the constant and unrelenting pressures we faced.

There are always going to be deaths; there are always going to be people affected by death from tragic circumstances. There will always be a need for a team of people to investigate the cause and manner of death, and to support those left behind. At that very moment, we were the team. We supported people in court as best we could.

Chapter 11

We supported families at the morgue. Most importantly, we supported each other. We did have another task however, one that proved to be always challenging and placed more stress on us than the all other tasks combined: the autopsy.

CHAPTER 12

LITTLE KNOWN FACTS ABOUT AUTOPSIES

I did a job once – no, I did this job a thousand times.

Most people are familiar with the term, autopsy. Television shows routinely mention them in passing. Some shows show the morgue where bodies are examined and cut open. The BBC's *Silent Witness* is one show that gets somewhat graphic in showing autopsies whereas *Midsomer Murders* tends to be 'more discreet'. At Glebe and previously at the Westmead morgue, the medical examination of a dead person is a procedure conducted by a specialist doctor called a forensic pathologist, assisted by a mortuary technician. The examination is a lengthy procedure and involves a number of steps.

As shown in most television shows, the body is laid on

Chapter 12

a steel examination table and is checked by the doctor for any external markings, bruises, injection sites or other signs that may be responsible for the person's death. The eyes are examined to look for any signs of small haemorrhaging. The pathologist records all findings. Photographs are sometimes taken. Incisions are made by the assistant. In most cases, this involves cutting behind the ears and slicing from there in a V shape to the base of the throat. A long incision is then made straight down the front of the torso, deviating around the navel, down towards the pubic area. The internal organs are then removed by the assistant in one large block and placed on an adjacent stainless steel table.

Specific organs are weighed, as the weight of an organ can inform the pathologist of any underlying illness or pathology. A heavy heart for example can potentially alert the pathologist to potential heart disease or high blood pressure. Heavy lungs may indicate heart failure. Small samples of organs are taken at this time and placed in small jars. These are later examined under the microscope. Some pathology is not always obvious to the naked eye and this process allows the medical staff to determine detailed specifics.

The doctor then makes an incision across the top of the head, slowly peeling away the skin on top of the skull. This is done by gently pulling the skin both towards the face and

Little known facts about autopsies

back towards the back of the neck. A small hand-held saw is used to remove the top of the skull enabling access to the brain cavity. The brain is removed and weighed and carefully examined. The brain and the internal organs are then placed back into the body and the assistant sews up the incisions.

In some cases, the brain is retained for more detailed examination. The brain is stored in a formalin mixture that causes it to harden. The brain is stored for up to ten days and then sliced and examined by a specialist doctor, a neuropathologist, who takes small samples from the brain and examines them under a microscope to look for any disease or pathology.

The Coronial Information and Support Team is responsible for informing the senior next of kin about the retention of the brain. If this is the case, one of my team would call the family and tell them that the brain had been retained for further examination – a really thankless task.

When I first started working at the morgue, it was common practice for the brain to be retained in nearly all cases. Brains would routinely be removed and kept for further testing. In those days, we didn't tell family members about this practice, unless asked. Clearly most people are unaware of many facets of an autopsy, so the practice remained until an independent investigation criticised this

Chapter 12

practice years later. The investigation highlighted a number of systemic failings in the area of organ retention amongst other findings. The Walker Report, as it is known, made a series of recommendations – one specifically mentioned the need for direct communication with the next of kin when organ retention occurred.

A decision was made to ensure that all families were informed when a whole organ was to be kept for further testing. The Coronial Information and Support Program was set up to liaise with families following retention of an organ to determine the cause of death. The unit also had other responsibilities but in many ways, this was its most vital function. Before the body was released for a funeral, my team would ring the family and explain the reasons for retention and the options the family could choose to make about burial with or without the retained organ.

Once an autopsy was conducted, we would receive an interim examination report, a report that contained the initial general findings, what further testing was required and whether whole organs had been retained. The reports usually came up from the laboratory by late morning as a rule. The team would meet and discuss each case and then we would divide the cases amongst each other to ensure equity. The decision to share the cases around the team meant that

Little known facts about autopsies

one person was not left with what was a really difficult task.

How do you tell someone that the brain or other whole organ of their loved one is to be retained? How can you tell the mother of a child, or the wife of a man to whom she has been married for many years? What of certain cultures and the need to respect their cultural mores? It was always challenging. There were some things none of us wished to do but this was our job.

In effect, we had to ensure that we provided the facts, and secondly to let the family know what options were available to them. The options were whether the body was to be kept at Glebe until the brain was returned to the body before release to a funeral home, or if they wanted the body released for burial or cremation without the brain. It was always a difficult conversation to have.

'Hello my name is John Merrick. I'm calling from the Coroner's office. I'm the coordinator of the Coronial Information and Support Program.' I would then make sure that I was speaking with the senior next of kin of the dead person before proceeding.

• • •

'I'm calling in relation to the autopsy that was conducted today by the doctor at Forensic Medicine. I believe you had

Chapter 12

a call from the counsellor informing you that it was being done today.'

'Yes, I had a call this morning from a lady telling me it was going to happen.'

'I just need to go through a few things about the report with you. Are you able to give me a few minutes now or is there someone else you would like me to speak to about this?'

'No, that's fine. I have time and I'm willing to listen to what you have to say.'

The woman I was speaking to on this occasion was the mother of a young man who had apparently died suddenly. He had a history of drug usage and had been diagnosed with epilepsy. The police had found drug paraphernalia near his body. According to friends, he had not used for some time but the circumstances surrounding his death indicated that drugs might have been a factor. The autopsy report had come back as undetermined. In other words, no clear cause of death had been established as yet. Blood tests and microscopic testing would determine the cause of death later. Blood samples would be sent to the Analytical Laboratories for drug testing. This process would often take weeks, sometimes months. The doctor had retained the brain because of his history of epilepsy. I was to tell the

Little known facts about autopsies

mother that the report was inconclusive as to the cause of death and, for this reason, more tests were required so the brain had been retained. She was a woman in her fifties, well spoken and anxious to hear what the report contained.

'Thank you, Mrs Smith. The examination was done by one of the specialist doctors today. He has done the initial investigation and I've received a copy of that report. Do you know what an autopsy is, Mrs Smith? Are you familiar with what happens and what the investigation entails?'

'No, I'm not, John. Do I need to know all the ins and outs? Is this important?'

'In this case I need you to understand a few very important things. We want to be as honest as possible with you. We want you to know as much as possible. So I guess the answer is yes, it is important that you understand all the facts.'

'All right, John. Thank you for being honest. Please tell me what was found and if you need to, tell me about the autopsy.' She sounded as though she really didn't want to hear too much only what might have caused her son's death but I had to make sure she understood about the brain retention.

'All right. The autopsy is like a big operation by a specialist doctor who initially examines the outside of his body, checking for bruises, bumps or anything else untoward.

Chapter 12

He then checks all the inside organs, examining them very carefully for any signs of illness or disease. When the doctor examines the organs, he keeps small tissue samples of each organ to check under the microscope at a later date. Sometimes what we can see with the naked eye isn't enough. A microscope can see things we can't. After this, we sew the body back up, you know like any operation. Is that clear so far?'

'Yes, I understand so far. It's very thorough, isn't it?' she added.

'Yes, it is. Now there is another series of tests they have to do. These include blood samples being taken away for testing. The samples will show up signs of any drugs or toxins in his system. We can determine the levels of drugs and such when these tests come back. It's like any pathology test that you may have had yourself.'

'Yes, I had one done last week. The results came back in a few days. Very quick these days.'

'Unfortunately, these tests take longer than that. They can take weeks, sometimes ten to twelve weeks.'

'Oh, that seems a very long time, John. Can they get any quicker?'

'Well, unfortunately a lot of people die and they have to, in a sense, wait in line. It is a long time, but the result will be

Little known facts about autopsies

made available to you when they return. Now at the moment, the interim results have come back from the autopsy and I'm sorry to say that the cause of death at the moment is pending toxicology testing and microscopic analysis. We haven't determined a cause of death yet.'

I went on. 'That can happen sometimes when the person is young and has had no recent history of serious illness. When there is no trauma to the body, sometimes we have to rely on other testing to establish a clear cause of death. So we'll have to wait for the blood tests to come back before we can provide the cause of death.'

'Oh, so I'll have to wait a long time to find out how he died?' she asked. 'The police told me they found some drug instruments near his body. I thought that he might have died from drugs. He was such a beautiful boy before he stared taking drugs; never any problem. He was such a gentle loving boy. He was an angel and then he went onto drugs in high school and he changed. He changed, John. He went from being so good to me to being rude and difficult. But I thought he had finished with the drugs. He told me he had not been taking them for nearly a year. He seemed happier with himself. He started his new job and he looked healthier and much better than he had for a long time. He came to see me most weeks. He even brought me a present

Chapter 12

last week …' She began to cry. 'I'm sorry, John. I don't mean to burden you with all my sadness.'

'That's ok, Mrs Smith. I understand it must be really hard for you at the moment. I hope you have someone to support you. It can be a really hard time.'

'Yes, my daughter is coming to stay with me for a week. She's coming from Queensland to stay. She's arriving tonight.'

'That's good to hear. I'm sure that you can support each other. Mrs Smith, there is one more thing I need to tell you. It's a difficult thing to hear and may be distressing for you. But as I said before, I have to be absolutely truthful with you. There is one more test that needs to be done; a test that needs to look at his history of epilepsy. When the doctor did the autopsy this morning, based on the fact he had epilepsy, he has decided to keep the brain. What this means is the brain is stored in a special chemical to harden it. Then it is cut very carefully and examined under a microscope. The reason we can't examine it this morning is that the brain is very soft and it needs to be kept until it hardens so the tests can be done. Does this make sense so far?'

'Oh well, I understand what you're saying but I don't want you to keep it. I want to bury him whole. I don't like that. There is no need. He hasn't had a fit in years. He had them

Little known facts about autopsies

when he was a boy but, as far as I know, he hasn't had one since he grew up. No, I don't want this test done. There's no need.'

'I'm sorry to say that the coroner feels as though this test is needed to determine the cause of his death. If the toxicology tests come back negative, we would then not know the cause of death. I'm sorry that the test has to proceed but the coroner has decided that it is vital.'

'That's awful. How can you just do what you want? What gives you the right to keep his brain? The brain is what makes someone who they are. It's their soul if you will. It's not right.' She went quiet. I knew this was such a hard thing to hear, telling a mother that we had kept her son's brain.

'I am sorry that I have had to break this news to you. I need to explain some options to you now I have told you. You see, you have a few choices to make and the decision will be yours. Firstly, you can elect to have your son released today and we will keep the brain here. That mean you can have the funeral whenever you wish and we will carry on doing the testing. The second option is we can keep him here until the testing is done and then replace the brain. After that, you can hold the funeral.'

'How long does that take?' she asked in a sharp fashion.

'About two weeks for the process to be finalised. I realise

Chapter 12

that's quite a long time to wait.'

'I can't wait that long. I have the funeral planned for next week. I can't alter people's plans. Some people need to take time off work. I can't change that now. Oh, this is terrible. I want to bury him whole.' She sounded so distressed by this stage.

'I understand Mrs Smith and I am sorry. It's not a decision that is taken lightly.'

'What happens to the brain after you finish the test. What do you do then?'

'It's cremated. When we finish the work, the brain is sent for cremation.'

'Well, in that case, I'll have the ashes collected and then place them with him. Can I do that?' she asked.

'I'm afraid not. You see when a brain is incinerated, there is nothing left. When people are cremated, it's the bones that produce the ashes. There are no bones within the brain. When it is incinerated, there is nothing left. I'm sorry.'

'You really don't give me any choice, do you? I don't have options here at all. You're keeping my son's brain and there's nothing I can do. I can't wait for two weeks. People will wonder about the delay. Oh, this is awful. I don't know how you people sleep at night. How can you do such terrible things? I'll speak to the funeral director and have

Little known facts about autopsies

him released. Mr Merrick, I wish you could understand my situation, but you won't. I hope really bad things happen to you. Good bye.'

With that, she hung up. I could understand the reasons for her anger. It would have been truly awful to receive a call such as this and be given such an awful choice – or as she said, no choice at all given the funeral timing had been arranged. I realised that the anger was a normal expression of her grief. She was distressed, powerless and, faced with this news, she had lashed out as much in despair as in anger. Many people did.

• • •

Generally, most people elect to have the body discharged as soon as possible for a funeral. It is different when young children die. Parents of young children usually want their child intact.

There was the case of the body of a seven-month-old baby girl being admitted to the morgue. The police report contained details that were disturbing. There were allegations of child abuse and the Department of Community Services had visited the home on a number of occasions. When the child was found dead, there were a few people in the family home. The home became a crime

Chapter 12

scene and the death was viewed as suspicious. One of the senior forensic pathologists had attended the home and felt that the child may have been shaken to death. The little body had bruises, not ones usually seen in a healthy child.

The pathologist came to see me. He informed me that he would be retaining the spinal cord, the eyes and the brain for further examination. I rang the investigating police officer and told her what the pathologist had said.

'Can we wait for a while before telling them? You know the child's death is being treated as suspicious, don't you?' she asked me.

'Yes, of course I do. I'm based here at the morgue and have been speaking with the pathologist.'

'Look, we know that someone in the house attacked and killed that kid. I want to know who did it and if we provide too much information too early, that could compromise the investigation. Can you wait a little longer?' she enquired.

'I can wait until late this afternoon. The autopsy is being done now so I'll have the interim report later today and I'll call you then. How does that suit?'

'That's great. I just need to put some things in place.' I knew what she meant. I'd be around long enough to realise that listening devices were going to be placed in the home so when I made the call, people might start talking and divulge

Little known facts about autopsies

something that may help the investigation. I didn't tell her I knew. I just let her think what she wanted to think.

I received the interim report later that day. The report indicated that the child had old fractures and bruising on her back and on her legs. The report expressed the view that the cause of death was Shaken Baby Syndrome. This finding was to be confirmed by examination of the spinal cord, the brain and the eyes. Shaken Baby Syndrome is not common. We see it infrequently. Basically, the child is shaken violently and this causes damage to the brain and the spinal cord. The shaking can also cause retinal bleeding, hence the need to retain the eyes. The only way to accurately diagnose this is by a thorough examination of all the organs.

I had no qualms about making this sort of call. I hated seeing children abused and was more than satisfied in helping gather evidence necessary to convict the perpetrator. I rang the police officer and told her I was ready to make the call to the mother of the child about the retained organs.

'Yes, that's fine, John. Go ahead and make the call. We have things in place now so call whenever you want.'

I made the call. I introduced myself to the mother of the child. I explained in general terms the purpose of the autopsy.

'So did she die of cot death,' the mother quizzed. She sounded tired.

Chapter 12

'It's too early to say at the moment but we do have preliminary findings that I need to discuss with you. Do you have time to talk now?'

'Sure, that's fine. What did she die from then? Was it the cough she had last week? Was it something else?'

'The report states that the interim finding is Shaken Baby Syndrome. Do you know what this means?'

'No. No I don't. What is it?'

'It means that the doctor thinks someone has shaken the child so much that the injuries have caused her death.' I was slow and deliberate in my words. I spoke at almost half speed so the words could not be misunderstood. 'Do you understand what I have just said?' I wanted to be sure that she fully comprehended my message.

'No, I don't know what you mean. I thought she died from cot death or something. So are you saying that she was shaken? Is that why she died?' Her voice began rising.

'Yes. That appears to be the situation. But we need to do other tests to confirm the findings so far. I have to tell you about the other tests we need to do. They involve us keeping some of her organs. I'd like to tell you about that now. Is that ok?'

'You mean someone shook her so hard she died?' She fell silent. 'He said she had gone to sleep. She'd been crying non-

Little known facts about autopsies

stop and she wouldn't shut up. I went in to try and settle her but she wouldn't stop. She just cried and cried. I came out and told Dave to take her but he said no. He just told me to shut her up. I went back in 'cos Dave was … a bit drunk. I tried again but she still cried, so I left her in there. She just went on and on so I had a cone and a couple of drinks. Dave went in and said he'd settle her. I didn't see him come out 'cos I fell asleep. You know, I was tired …'

'Yes, I understand. She wouldn't settle so Dave went in at some stage to settle her. Is that right?'

'Yes, but Dave would never hurt her. He's smacked her sometimes when she's been naughty but that's all. I'm sure he wouldn't shake her. You think maybe you've got the wrong result? Could your tests be wrong?'

How could anyone smack a seven-month-old child, I thought. That's just abuse. Some people shouldn't have kids. I quickly dismissed the thought.

'I guess we'll have to wait and see when the results come back. But I need to go back and tell you about the tests and the organs we need to keep for testing. It's important I tell you so you can understand.'

'Oh right. Ok, go ahead.'

'This is not easy for you to hear and I am sorry for being so blunt with you. We have retained the brain for further

Chapter 12

testing. We need to keep it to check it thoroughly under a microscope. We have also kept the spinal cord and I'm sorry to tell you we have kept both of her eyes. I'm really sorry to tell you this.'

'So you're telling me you kept her eyes and her brain? What the fuck did you keep them for? You can't do that to her. That's wrong. What the fuck!' she exploded. 'You're not going to do this. We'll stop you. This isn't right. You can't do this.' She had become overcome with emotion. She screamed at me. 'You pricks think you can do anything. Well, you're not going to get away with this. I'll stop you.'

'I know you're angry with me. I can understand that but the fact is the tests need to be done because someone has deliberately shaken your daughter and caused her death. Now I know you're upset with me. What about the person who has done this to her? What do think about that? Were there other people at your place that night, or just you and Dave?' She stopped screaming but I could hear her breathing heavily on the end of the phone.

'There was Jason and Megan who were there for a while. Jason got the nods and last I saw he fell asleep. Megan was off her tree. She was pissed before she arrived and drank some more, then fell asleep on the couch. Dave was having a few cones and drinking a bit. The last time I saw Dave,

Little known facts about autopsies

he went in and was going to settle Amy. But it couldn't be Dave. He wouldn't do that. I know him. He's cranky with her sometimes but I don't think he would shake her.' She became less hostile to me and stopped shouting. She almost became reflective. I could hear her throwing thoughts around in her head as to what had happened to the little girl.

'I have some things I need you to think about. I've told you about the organs. You have a choice to make here. Now we can allow her release from here tomorrow if you like. You can speak to any funeral director you wish and they will speak to us here. We can then release her but without those organs. Or you can choose to let her stay here until we finish the testing and then we can replace the organs back into her body. That's likely to take a couple of weeks.'

'You know I can live with the brain being taken but I can't live with the thought of her having no eyes. I can't bear that. She had lovely eyes. They were real cute. I can't bear that. Can you keep her there until you put them back in? That will give me time to speak to the funeral people. So keep her there for the next couple of weeks. Can I ask you a question? Do you put the eyes back where they came from? You know, back where they're supposed to be?'

I dreaded that question. 'We can't put them back in place in the eye sockets. I'm sorry but that's not possible. We will

Chapter 12

place them back in her body but not the eye sockets.'

'Where in the body? Where do you put my daughter's eyes?' Her voice was rising again.

'It's not possible to put them back where they were previously. Eyes are attached by tissue. When the autopsy is done, tissue is removed and examined. The eyes can no longer be attached in the same way as before. We place them back into her body cavity.' I had told the truth. We couldn't place them back in the same location. The eyes would also be dissected and would not resemble her daughter's eyes after the testing was done.

'Oh, that's so terrible. I wish I could see her little face again and have her open her eyes and laugh. She was a cheeky kid …' She stopped then started talking again. 'Dave is here. I'm going to get going. I need to speak to him. So you keep her for the next while and I'll speak with the funeral people. Ok, Bye.' The next second she was gone. I replaced the handset. I looked around my office and to the picture on my desk of Helen and I thought of our kids. Someone had shaken a little girl to death. I felt for the little girl whose life had been cut short. I thought of my kids and the life they had. There was no comparison.

The phone rang a few seconds later. It was the police officer working the case. 'Thanks, John. That was great.

Little known facts about autopsies

She's got the information and Dave has just arrived. I'll have to wait and see what the next conversation is about. Thanks again. Appreciate the help.' The conversation was less than ten seconds.

I learned later that Dave was charged with Amy's murder. It was as Amy's mother had suggested. Dave was tired and affected by substances. He couldn't keep her quiet, so he shook her so hard, she died. It's as simple and horrific as that.

• • •

Calls to families about the retention of brains or other whole organs are always fraught. People are often devastated to hear the news. Often they cannot understand why the decision has been made. It appears to them to make no sense. Sometimes, people argue that retention is contrary to their religious beliefs. Many feel that their dead relative would not be whole in death and fail to find the afterlife. Without something as important as the brain, what would happen to them after death? How would they cope? People cried, screamed, and threatened us on numerous occasions. We received calls from politicians advocating for their constituents, calls from media outlets, lawyers representing the families, all asking, pleading, threatening us and wanting

Chapter 12

us to reverse the decision. I explained to many of them they could take their concerns to the Supreme Court. They of course had every right to do so. Most in fact accepted the situation grudgingly.

To this day, I deeply regret upsetting so many family members. I understand and accept that they were distressed and angry and had to lash out at the messenger. The decision to retain was never mine. Still, the team accepted the angry tirades that came our way. We became accustomed to the response.

While generally we all accept and understand the forensic procedures surrounding death, many are not fully aware of the types of testing that need to take place to reach a finding. While this book many help to increase understanding about the procedures required, it does not take away the raw emotions when faced with the news of what might happen to their deceased loved one.

The very idea that the brain has been removed from someone you love is horrifying, The news that the very part of the body that makes them unique, that makes them who they are, has been taken and may not be available for the burial is doubtless a huge shock. Asking a relative to make an informed decision about whether to bury without the brain in such a short space of time is almost cruel. On

Little known facts about autopsies

many occasions however, without a careful examination of the organ, it is impossible to determine the cause of death with any accuracy.

Sometimes retaining the brain helps those family members who are still living. On occasions, the examination discovers pathology within the brain that may be a warning to those left behind – discoveries that enable family to seek treatment and increase their chances of a long life.

The changes to practices that led to families being informed about retained body parts were important: everyone has the right to know what had happened and why decisions were made. It may have been kinder when families were not informed. Despite the trauma the information can cause, we now know that to deny people this knowledge is neither acceptable nor ethical.

• • •

Shaken baby syndrome does not always lead to death. Mild shaking of a baby is also dangerous so that even if the baby doesn't show any symptoms at the time, they can develop learning or behavioural problems later on.

- Some signs and symptoms include:
- extreme irritability
- difficulty staying awake

Chapter 12

- breathing problems
- tremors and vomiting
- seizures, paralysis
- coma and death.

CHAPTER 13

A FEW MORE TALES

I have told you about bus crashes, terrorist bombings, suicides and other tragedies. I would like to leave you with a couple more snapshots of my other memories of the morgue before I sign off; a few short snippets of vivid recollections that spring to mind.

Undercover

We stood on a sloping hillside looking down at the prison complex which sprawled out neatly in clear geometric patterns. Two police officers and I stood looking towards the prison. The police had sent in a witness to speak to a prime suspect in the case of a disappearance of a young girl many years prior. Listening devices had been used to monitor the conversation. The suspect was serving time for previous paedophile-related crimes. The witness, a brave

Chapter 13

woman, was to go inside and try to raise the issue of the young girl's disappearance in an attempt to get the suspect to open up and confess his crimes. Unfortunately, the devices did not bear fruit. In the absence of him talking about the victim, there was little more that could be done. Very disappointed, the three of us stood there wondering what to do next.

'Well, it didn't work. We just lucked out. He didn't mention her name once. Not one word. We might be wasting our time. Do we go again? Is it worth the risk? How's our witness doing, John? Do you think she can still do it?'

'Yeah, I think so. She's a tough lady and she's really keen to help. Maybe one more shot might do it,' I said in hope more than expectation. 'I'll speak to her and see how she feels. She's tired now but give her some time and she might be alright.'

'Maybe. What if we try something else? What if we try to get someone in to talk to him and get him to open up? You know, someone that he feels he can confess to, maybe a counsellor, a padre. He might want to confess what he's done if he feels he's safe doing it, John.' He said looking straight at me. 'Feel like going in undercover as a padre, get him to talk. What do you think? Worth a shot?'

To this day I'm not sure whether he was serious or not.

A few more tales

Maybe he was. I didn't answer. My thoughts immediately ran to the spy movies I had seen James Bond undercover stuff. I saw myself getting a confession from the villain and running out to make sure he faced justice. That thought lasted about two seconds.

'No thanks, mate. I'd end up getting buggered senseless and no confession. But hey, thanks for the offer.'

The police did manage to get their man eventually. He was convicted of the girl's death and is currently still serving a lengthy term.

Cerebral anoxia

A young man was found inside a car in a clearing in a national park. The engine was off. He had a plastic garbage bag around his head and his hands were loosely tied to the steering wheel of the car. There was a rubber hose leading from a cylinder into a small hole in the garbage bag. The cylinder contained helium. It was a cylinder hired from a party shop to inflate balloons at parties. None of us had ever seen this before and were intrigued as to how he had found out about this method to take his own life. There were no suspicious circumstances surrounding the death but the method was unusual.

I spoke to one of the forensic doctors who explained that

Chapter 13

helium displaces oxygen. In the absence of oxygen, a person would gradually pass out and since the helium would be trapped in the bag and the gas would still keep entering, he would die from cerebral anoxia, a lack of oxygen to the brain.

We discovered a website that effectively says that humans are ruining the planet. Its message was simple. Kill yourself. It advocated people taking their own lives to prevent the world from being overpopulated. One of the methods recommended on the site was precisely the method employed by this man. It went through step-by-step instructions on how to kill yourself using a helium cylinder, a garbage bag and some tubing. The site still functions to this day although I believe that the method of helium ingestion no longer features on the site.

Voices raised in anger

I rarely raised my voice to my team. Occasionally, we would disagree but this was done in a relatively friendly way. We understood each other and did our best to make a difficult job a little easier.

This particular year, my brother was getting married just before Christmas. Of course, Helen and I attended and thoroughly enjoyed ourselves. I had had a fair amount of red wine to salute my brothers' wedding. I carried a pager

A few more tales

as always in the days prior to mobile phones. I didn't think much about it because one of my team was on call. She would respond to any need. The wedding reception had finished and I was near home when the pager buzzed. It said to ring Glebe urgently. Must be some sort of mistake, I thought. They probably don't realise that my colleague is on call. I arrived home and called work. I knew the assistant who answered. 'Hi, it's John. You know that my colleague is on call, don't you.'

'Yep, I do. We've had a plane crash and there are some families here to do the identifications. We have three groups here and I need you to come in.'

'What happened to …?' I didn't even get to say her name.

'She's here.'

'So why are you calling me then?'

'She's really pissed. She's not fit to see the families. I think she's had too many cocktails.' He tried to sound light hearted but it wasn't working.

'Oh God, I'm still half pissed from my brother's wedding. I've just got back home now. I'll have a mate drive me in.' This was mandatory as I was too drunk to drive. I asked Dave, a friend, to drive me to Glebe as soon as possible. Never shirking a challenge, Dave got me there in quick time. I stuck my head out the window on the way in a vain

Chapter 13

attempt to sober up as best I could. I chewed gum to try to hide the effects of the wine. I was still drunk when I arrived. I went straight to the car park, anxious to avoid the families on the footpath outside the rear door. I wanted to get some background details on the crash to find out more before seeing any family members.

I went to the office and saw my colleague looking even worse than I did. She was sitting on a chair in the office and looking rather sheepish as I walked in.

'What the hell do you think you're doing?' I blazed at her forgetting for a moment there were families outside in the waiting room adjacent to the office. 'I ask one thing only – stay sober when on call and look at you. What happened?' I asked more out of anger than any real desire to know. 'Well, what the hell happened?'

'I just had one cocktail too many. I was having drinks with friends and I thought that …' She was searching for words.

'You didn't think at all. I'm so angry with you. Get a damn cab home now! We will talk more about this tomorrow. You're in big trouble. Go on, just go home.' I raised my voice at her again. Not my best efforts in staff management. I was too angry with her and I should have not have raised my voice especially when I was as inebriated. I was just angry at my evening off work being rudely interrupted. She walked off towards the car park to go through the front door. She didn't look back.

'Sorry' I said to the assistant who was witness to my tirade.

'No, you're right. I hate to break this to you but we still have three families here from the crash. Can we do something about that now rather than spend more time kicking arse?'

He went on to briefly explain what had happened. The first body was already in the viewing room so I went in to check on the state of the body as I always did. I closed the sliding door behind me as I made my way towards the door into the foyer. All right here goes, I thought. I entered the foyer to see a couple of people. A man and a woman in their fifties were seated on armchairs, holding hands for physical as much as emotional support it seemed. The man stood as I approached.

'Hello, I'm John, the counsellor here. I am very sorry I kept you waiting for so long. I had to travel from some distance. I'm sorry for keeping you such a long time. I know you're anxious to see him, I'm sure.'

I'm sure I smelled of alcohol at the time. When you have drunk too much, you can't smell it on yourself but others can smell it on you, especially when you are talking to them. I now wonder what they must have thought; two counsellors clearly affected by alcohol and dealing with the

Chapter 13

aftermath of a plane crash. If they did notice, they didn't let on. I accompanied them into the anteroom and prepared them for the viewing. The issue of inebriation was never mentioned again.

I finished seeing all the families early on Sunday morning. We had managed to muddle through. The counsellor who had been drinking while on call left the job soon after. Our relationship was never the same after that episode. I may have been harsh on her and part of me regrets my actions, particularly shouting at her. She moved on and opened a business elsewhere. Maybe that was more to her taste.

Recognising the dead ... or not

I received a call one day from a police sergeant I knew. After the usual round of greetings, his voice turned serious. 'It's about that woman who passed away the other day. I just need to give you some extra information. You know one of your own.'

'Sorry, what do you mean one of our own. I don't get it.'

'You know' he insisted, 'the girl that died the other day from Leichhardt, the one who worked there.'

'Sorry, mate. I don't understand. We haven't had anyone who worked here die recently. What are you on about?' I was confused. He sounded genuine but I don't remember anyone

A few more tales

dying that I knew and who had come to Glebe and certainly not in the last few days.

'Her name is Taylor,' he insisted.

I looked down the list of recent deaths on the computer.

'No. There's no one here by that name.' I was relieved. He had been mistaken.

'That's because you have her maiden name, not her married name.' He told me the other name. I stopped in shock. I hadn't known her well. She had been here on a locum position. A quiet woman, I remembered her as being quite friendly with a nice smile. I looked at the name and dived into the file to get more details. We had done an autopsy on her. She was still at the morgue, not yet released to a funeral director. I rang downstairs to the mortuary office.

'Do me a favour, please? I need a body bag on one of the bodies opened please.' I gave the person the name of the deceased. 'I just need to see her for a second. Cheers.'

I rushed downstairs and opened the sliding door to the body storage area. The trolley had been pulled out from its space amongst the rows of trollies. The body bag was unzipped but still covered her. I pulled the plastic away to see her face. She was damp, her hair was still wet from washing after the autopsy. Her eyes were closed. I could see the autopsy sutures. I looked hard at her, as if trying to

Chapter 13

recognise her. The angle was all wrong.

I tilted my head so I could get a better look in a hope to recognise her. Still, I failed to recognise a woman I had seen and talked with recently. At that height on the trolley, and with her lying horizontal, it was hard to recognise her. It's interesting but true that we rarely interact with people when they are lying down. The only people in our lives with whom we do are those closest to us; those with whom we share intimacy. I looked again, anxious to verify it was her. It had to be her. This woman looked the same age and shared features but I wasn't sure. I closed the bag and asked the assistant to replace the security tag.

I went upstairs to speak to the senior forensic pathologist who had done the autopsy. He would have to know if it was her body as he had worked with her quite closely during her time working at the morgue.

I entered his room and told him about the call. I told him I had been downstairs to see her but that I could not recognise her. We both went downstairs and reopened the bag. Both he and I looked at her from different angles. There was nothing that we could see that helped us to recognise the body as the woman we had both worked with.

'I can't believe I was talking to her last week,' he said, 'and then I'm doing an autopsy on her a week later and I don't even

A few more tales

give her a second glance. And even if I had, I don't think I would have recognised her. We're looking now and still can't see the resemblance.' He was clearly upset.

It was astonishing to me to know that we had done an autopsy on someone we had all known, even if only for a short time, and yet we didn't recognise her – even the pathologist who had done the autopsy. It occurred to me that those who work on the dead don't see the person – they see only the body in an effort to find out what it was that caused the death. We only see a job that needs to be done. Then we move onto the next job. It is as simple, and as horrible, as that.

CHAPTER 14

WALKING OUT OF THE MORGUE

In 2009, I was working with a great team. We had experience within the team and a great sense of camaraderie. We worked hard, attended inquests around New South Wales, and made calls to families about inquests and investigations. We often lectured professional groups about the coronial system. We were given the opportunity to consult with other countries in their development of coronial jurisdiction. The relationship with all the coroners was very positive. We felt in many ways that we were making a difference.

On a personal level, I felt settled too but even so, something kept gnawing away at me. I asked myself some serious questions. Could I see myself working here until retirement? Would I finish work one day and then get

Chapter 14

wheeled in downstairs the next to the body storage area? Was there more to life than the morgue at the State Coroner's office? Did I want to work day in, day out with dead people for the rest of my working life?

I began to look at other options for employment, not with any great sense of urgency to move on, but just to see what was out there. One day I saw a job – Unit Head of Social Work at a major Sydney teaching hospital. It felt like I hadn't been in social work for a thousand years but I had lectured at numerous hospitals and had recently lectured at this particular one. I had a vision of working close to home (the hospital was very close), no more long commutes to work or trips away up country for inquests that left Helen to look after the kids. So, I put together an application and went for the job. I had visions of nurturing younger social workers all anxious to learn and develop their knowledge. It sounded like an interesting job and I felt that I could definitely contribute. The hospital did too. To my absolute surprise, I got the job. After twenty years of my life, I walked out of the morgue on my own terms.

I soon discovered that life away from the Coroner's office was very different. During my time in the Coroner's Court and in 'the morgue' which we always referred to as 'Forensics', I dealt with many types of people, right across the

Walking out of the morgue

board. I mixed with police, magistrates, journalists, writers, counsellors, members of the legal profession, people from all walks of life, family members of the deceased, ambassadors, state and federal politicians and murderers – all sorts of people. I spoke with these men and women at different times often in times of crisis when they were distressed, upset, angry. I attended crime scenes where bodies were still in situ. My language varied but when I dealt with my team, we tended to swear a lot. When I spoke with the police, I swore a lot. When I spoke with some groups, well, I swore a lot. When I spoke with the families of the deceased, I didn't swear. I was considered, listening and offering support. But generally, in most situations, I swore a lot. You get the picture. That was the way I talked (and did many others who worked with me at the morgue). It was my usual means of communicating. Vulgar, maybe; habitual, absolutely.

I attended a meeting during the first month in my new job at the hospital. I can't remember the specifics of the matter, but it was about the safety of patients and staff on a ward where something had arisen. I attended the ward accompanied by one of my team, a woman in her late twenties. The discussion ensued. I said my piece punctuating my sentences with my usual expletives; a few f's here, a couple of other expletives there. I thought nothing of it and

Chapter 14

walked away satisfied with the solution.

Then I noticed my colleague who looked rather ashen faced. 'It went pretty well, don't you think?' I suggested. She nodded but qualified her agreement.

'John, you know you can't speak that way. You can't swear all the time like that. It's unprofessional.'

I hadn't even noticed that I had been swearing that much, that's how habitual it had become. I just did it. I thought that maybe she was overreacting but didn't say so at the time.

After a while, a number of staff mentioned my swearing requesting that I not speak that way. I tried to change my ways, but the more I tried, the more I disliked the political correctness of the situation. I worked hard, anxious to make a difference.

I carried what was known as the roster book. I also carried a pager. Some areas of the hospital were not covered by a dedicated social worker so when a ward was in need of a social worker, I allocated the case to whoever was next on the list. Although everyone was on the list, the extra work was most unwelcome. I thought one thing I could do was to take these cases myself. So I took many of them to save the team from having to pick them up.

I enjoyed the work but the meetings were, well, not what I had expected. I had witnessed some bullying there, and one time another health professional made the mistake of trying to bully me. I had seen her bully others and I was not prepared to back down. I explained the situation in no uncertain terms. 'You honestly think your 1950s management style and the look on your face is going to intimidate me. What are you going to do? Punch me?' She never tried it again.

I didn't miss the work at the Coroner's office. Well, maybe I did. I really missed some of the people. While I had been excited to get the new job, I soon realised that the hospital system may not be for me. Some of the team were great, professional dedicated people willing to go the extra mile. Others, well, could I see myself staying until retirement? I didn't think so. I stayed for nearly three years and then moved on.

It doesn't really matter where I went next. I went to another job where the money was fine, the job enjoyable. I left there a while back and now I'm working as a counsellor. Back where it all began. I love counselling. It's my passion.

In some respects, I have found it hard on occasions to move on from the work I did at the Coroner's office. I tell myself that it's pointless looking back. Best to focus on what can be changed. Invest in the future. One old friend from Forensics told me that I would have difficulty moving on. He said that I might go from job to job at some pace before settling again.

Chapter 14

He warned me that if this happened, I should ring him and we could talk. I value his advice and sage wisdom much of the time. On other occasions, I just ignore him.

During the writing of this book I have told you about some of my experiences. When I first started working at Glebe in 1989, I was young, enthusiastic and willing to embrace all challenges. I thought I had the world at my feet. The work excited me. I felt that I was making a difference in people's lives. I felt that I could singlehandedly make a huge difference – I could really help those bereaved by sudden death.

I sometimes reflect on who I was at the time and who I have become. I know that my time within this environment changed me. I don't think it was merely the passage of time that has turned me into who I am today. The changes within me are shaped by many things, many events and many relationships. I developed numerous friendships over my time at the Glebe morgue. I became close to fellow counsellors, police officers and magistrates. Some of the friendships I made are still going strong to the present day. I became close to people, people I had met as their counsellor. The relationships deepened over time. Some might criticise me for developing friendships with bereaved family members. I hold firm in my belief that I have done no harm by having these friendships. I care for these friends as much as they care for me.

Conversely, I think I have become more callous too. I am not moved in the same way as I was previously. I think that seeing so many people in tears and agony over the years did have an impact. I developed a thick skin so I could be as professional as I could manage to be. I needed to do this to stay focussed and offer as much help as I was able.

At times in viewings, I would stand at the rear of the room watching a devastated human being cry at the sight of their dead loved one. I was unmoved many times. The process became a cognitive exercise for me. I didn't feel so much as think. I learned techniques over the years that helped the bereaved person to gain insight, to learn to accept the emotions they had. I learned techniques to support the living in their own expressions of grief, to accept their own sadness and traumatic reactions. I became acutely aware of people's reactions to death. This acuity helped me to help them. In some ways, if I had had more emotional reactions, they may have got in the way of helping them deal with their own loss. Yes, I have hardened. I don't make friends easily. I lost good friends during my time at the Coroner's, some through differences of opinion, some through differences in ambition, others through choice. It happens to us all. We have friends at different times and then we move on.

POSTSCRIPT

I know that some of this book will resonate with you, the reader. You may have had a loss of your own and some of the elements within the book may bring back memories. Maybe I met you at some time when you lost a friend or family member. You might think that I'm not a bad person. I know that some chapters may have you believe that I am someone who is thoughtless in the least or guilty of cruelty due to my seemingly offhand attitude to my job dealing with the dead. I accept all of the charges, Your Honour. I am guilty of all charges. I am a man who has done both good and bad. I have done my best at times and, at other times, I have been completely derelict in my duty of care. You see, I am both the architect and the victim of my circumstances. I helped people when they were at their most vulnerable. I have spent hundreds and hundreds of hours being with people viewing their

Postscript

deceased loved ones, often holding them in my arms as they cried and were absolutely disconsolate.

I spent time in a culture that I helped create. The black humour and practical jokes juxtaposed with the horror of sudden and unnatural death. I cringe at my thoughtlessness during times when I was trying to be funny and ended up being exceedingly cruel. However, the raw nature of grief in the aftermath of death is an area in which I felt at peace. I realised that I could help; that is what I tried to do. I failed at it sometimes but mostly I feel that I helped those who survive the death of those whom they love the most. As it is in many areas of life, we try to do what is right but sometimes fail. I believe that my ability to help has far outweighed my failings. I hope so. I hope that the sum total of my experience in the Glebe morgue, working as a forensic counsellor, is something that I can look back on in my dotage with a measure of satisfaction and a sense of a job well done.

John

ACKNOWLEDGEMENTS

Many people have made this book a reality. My heartfelt thanks to my patient wife, Helen, who put up with me and supported me during my writing. To my sons who actively encouraged me in my endeavours.

To Monique Butterworth, my publisher, who encouraged me to write in the first place and to Susie Stevens, my amazing editor who transformed my ramblings into something I hope you will enjoy.

ABOUT THE AUTHOR

John Merrick is a social worker by trade, having graduated from the University of New South Wales in 1983.

John has worked in the public and private sectors and has taught crisis counselling around the country which included how to cope with bereavement, suicide, disaster response and how to debrief those who are affected by crises.

During his time at the Coroner's Court in Glebe, John learnt much about bereavement and how to help those going through this difficult time. He also learnt many life lessons that he has been able to share with others in both his professional and private life.

Currently, John is working as a counsellor in a large company in Sydney.

A singing tragic, John still plays in a rock-n-roll band belting out tunes from last century. John lives with his wife, Helen, in Sydney and has three grown sons, all of whom give him enormous pride.

First published in 2017 by New Holland Publishers
Sydney

Level 1, 178 Fox Valley Road, Wahroonga, NSW 2076, Australia

newhollandpublishers.com

Copyright © 2022 New Holland Publishers
Copyright © 2017 in text: John Merrick
Copyright © 2017 in images: Cover, Shutterstock; Page 237, John Merrick

All rights reserved. No part of this publication may be reproduced, stored in a retrieval system or transmitted, in any form or by any means, electronic, mechanical, photocopying, recording or otherwise, without the prior written permission of the publishers and copyright holders.

The author has recreated events, locales and conversations from his memories of them. To maintain anonymity in some instances names have been changed to protect the privacy of individuals. Christine Simpson and Gunther Deix have given permission to use their names in telling the story Ebony's death and setting up the Homicide Victims Support Group.

A record of this book is held at the National Library of Australia.

ISBN 9781921024795

Managing Director: Fiona Schultz
Publisher: Monique Butterworth
Project Editor: Susie Stevens
Cover and Layout Design: Andrew Quinlan
Production Director: Arlene Gippert

10 9 8 7 6 5 4 3 2

Keep up with New Holland Publishers:
NewHollandPublishers
@newhollandpublishers

www.ingramcontent.com/pod-product-compliance
Lightning Source LLC
Chambersburg PA
CBHW070631160426
43194CB00009B/1429